HUGO

Find, Identity, Gather, Prepare, and Cook Edible Wild Plants, Insects, and Select Animals Safely in the Wild

FORAGING

41 TECHNIQUES & STRATEGIES TO SURVIVE THE OUTDOORS THROUGH FORAGING

© **Copyright 2024 - All rights reserved.**

The content contained within this book may not be reproduced, duplicated, or transmitted without direct written permission from the author or the publisher.

Under no circumstances will any blame or legal responsibility be held against the publisher, or author, for any damages, reparation, or monetary loss due to the information contained within this book. Either direct or indirect. You are responsible for your own choices, actions, and results.

<u>Legal Notice:</u>

This book is copyright protected. This book is only for personal use. You cannot amend, distribute, sell, use, quote, or paraphrase any part of the content within this book. without the consent of the author or publisher.

<u>Disclaimer Notice:</u>

Please note the information contained within this document is for educational and entertainment purposes only. All effort has been executed to present accurate, up-to-date, and reliable complete information No warranties of any kind are declared or implied. Readers acknowledge that the author is not engaging in the rendering of legal, financial, medical, or professional advice. The content within this book has been derived from various sources. Please consult a licensed professional before attempting any techniques outlined in this book.

By reading this document the reader agrees that under no circumstances as the author is responsible for any losses, direct or indirect. which are incurred as a result of the use of the information contained within this document, including, but not limited to, – errors. omissions, or inaccuracies

Table of Contents

Introduction 5

Chapter 1: Foraging Fundamentals 7
 History of Foraging 7
 Different Methods of Foraging 10
 Key Principles of Foraging 11
 The Importance of Foraging 13
 Other Benefits of Foraging 15
 Safety Precautions 17

Chapter 2: Plant Identification Skills 23
 Importance 23
 Challenges of Identifying Plants 25
 Mastering Plant Identification 27
 Universal Edibility Test 33
 Seasonal Foraging 35
 Activity: Plant Bingo 38

Chapter 3: Medicinal Plant Foraging 41
 Uses of Medicinal Plants 41
 Common Medicinal Plants 43
 Ways to Prepare and Use Medicinal Plants 47
 Exercise: Creating Your Own Herbal Infusion 49

Chapter 4: Protein-Rich Foraging 51
 Why Do Humans Need Protein? 51
 Insects as a Source of Protein 52
 Identifying Edible Insects 56
 Tips for Foraging insects 58
 Foraging Eggs 61

Chapter 5: Fungi 67
A Closer Look on Fungi 68
Types of Fungi 68
Uses of Fungi 71
Foraging Fungi Safely 73
How to Cook and Prepare Foraged Fungi..................81
Exercise: Fungi Spore Print Making............................83

Chapter 6: Water Resource Foraging.............................. 85
Aquatic Plant Foraging...85
Foraging Aquatic Creatures 93
Finding drinking water 94
Exercise: Survive the Wilderness...............................100

Chapter 7: Environment-Specific Foraging 103
Forests and Woodlands 104
Coastal Regions 108
Urban Landscapes...110
Exercise: Foraging Scavenger Hunt...........................113

Chapter 8: Sustainable Foraging 115
Why Sustainable Foraging Matters 116
Principles of Ethical Foraging 118
Understanding Foraging Laws 119
Practicing Conservation and Rehabilitation...........121
Interacting with Wildlife..124

Conclusion 127

Techniques Recap 131

Resources 135

Exclusive Bonuses 139

Introduction

As concrete jungles and digital distractions surround a majority of people, many cannot recognize an edible plant, even if it is growing right in their backyards. That's a problem. A big one. What happens when the grocery stores are empty or when you need to find food in an emergency?

In our modern, technologically-driven world, you've lost that innate knowledge our ancestors relied on for survival. You've disconnected from nature, unable to recognize the bounty of food, medicine, and resources available right outside your door. This leaves you vulnerable, especially in situations where conventional food sources are unavailable or unsustainable. Through the chapters of this book, I seek to help you rekindle that connection and equip you with the knowledge and skills to forage for survival, sustenance, or pleasure.

In the pages of this book, you'll rediscover the ancient tradition of foraging. You'll start by learning to identify edible and medicinal plants. I won't stop at plants, though. There's an entire world of protein-rich food aside from the usual meat. Together, I help you decode the art of sourcing and identifying these resources. And, since humans can't survive on food alone, I'll also touch upon water resource foraging, mastering not only the techniques to locate and purify it but also to forage the aquatic plants and marine creatures.

As you delve deeper, I'll take you on a journey through various environments, each with its unique palette of edible flora and fauna. And most importantly, you'll learn to forage sustainably, nurturing the very environment that nourishes you. By the end of this book, you won't just be a forager; you'll become a steward of nature.

With each new chapter, you'll gain valuable skills and form a profound connection with the natural world. You will find 41 techniques, tips, and strategies equipping you with foraging knowledge and skills peppered throughout the entire book. It's intentionally designed this way to serve as your guide along each step of the process. With each foraging adventure, I promise you'll understand why our ancestors revered nature and realize the incredible abundance Earth provides.

This book is brimming with insights from countless years of embracing the wild. Recalling the hurdles from my initial years of this lifestyle, I'm eager to pass on my learnings to help you develop the necessary skills you can use, even in survival situations. This is my token of gratitude to the community that has enriched my life enormously. If these insights can make a difference and save even a single life, then every bit of effort has been worthwhile.

However, this book can also be your guide if you ever desire to rediscover the bounties of the Earth or merely seek an engaging hobby. With so many species, each with their unique attributes, it's understandable if you don't know where to begin. The web of life that binds all creatures together, including us humans, is awe-inspiring but can seem intimidating. As a naturalist and outdoor enthusiast, I've too have felt overwhelmed when I was first starting out.

My passion for understanding and fascination with the intricate connections between man and the environment led me to document and teach about the lost art of foraging. I am eager to share these insights with you, so let's begin!

Chapter 1
Foraging Fundamentals

Far from the towering supermarket aisles and bustling farmer's markets, nature's pantry lies in wait, teeming with diverse, delicious, and nutritious ingredients. In the increasingly industrialized world, foraging re-establishes an essential link between humans and the land, reviving an ancient practice that was once integral to survival. This chapter sets the foundation for your foraging journey, equipping you with the critical knowledge and tools to embark on this rewarding endeavor.

You'll travel back in time to explore the rich history and underlying principles of foraging, understand why it truly matters, and learn important tips to ensure your foraging adventure is safe and respectful to the environment. This isn't just about teaching you the ins and outs of foraging; it's about inviting you on a journey. A journey to reconnect with nature, reignite the wisdom of our ancestors, and rediscover the joy of finding food in its purest form. The importance of foraging extends beyond sustenance; it's a profound, almost spiritual, connection with the world around you.

History of Foraging

At the very essence of human survival lies the ancient art of foraging – a quest for sustenance that has unfolded since our first ancestors walked this planet. Primordial humans were navigating the labyrinth of Mother Nature, their survival tied to the vital clues whispered by the earth beneath their feet and the canopy above. They hunted for plump, vibrant berries hidden under leaves, deciphered the secret language of aromatic herbs pushing through the soil, and braved the buzzing guard of bees to retrieve honey, a liquid gold concealed within the rough bark of trees. For our ancestors, each sunrise brought forth a new chapter in their ongoing quest for survival, and foraging was the lifeline woven into every page.

During the Ice Age, as vast ice sheets transformed landscapes, early humans foraged for robust roots and hardy tubers that thrived beneath the frozen surface. In the rich, green cradle of the tropics, they scaled trees for fruit and nuts while coastal communities plumbed the salty depths of the sea, harvesting a bounty of shellfish and seaweed. The art of foraging was far more than a meal ticket – it was an intricate dance of survival choreographed by the shifting rhythms of seasons and the often harsh conditions of the environment.

As these early humans walked the trails of survival, they honed their skills, decoding the language of plants and animals. They discovered that the fallen petals of a flower signaled the ripening of fruit, the skittering path of insects led to hidden plant bulbs, and the circling birds of prey in the sky often unveiled a potential feast on the ground. Like detectives, they pieced together a fascinating jigsaw puzzle where every creature and plant were interconnected pieces leading to nourishment.

But foraging extended beyond mere sustenance. It was a deeply social and cultural activity, serving as a conduit for wisdom passed down through generations. Traditional lore, wrapped around each plant or fungi, was shared through stories and recipes. This wisdom, often held by elders, guided each new generation, shaping a symbiotic relationship with the environment that respected natural cycles and honored sustainability.

As societies evolved, agriculture gradually nudged foraging to the sidelines. But the practice never completely faded, resurfacing during challenging times. For instance, consider World War II, when city-dwellers planted "Victory Gardens" and foraged for wild foods to supplement their scarce rations. Here foraging became an emblem of resilience, a testament to human adaptability, demonstrating that when traditional food systems falter, the wild can offer sustenance.

Today, foraging is witnessing a vibrant resurgence. With a growing consciousness about the environmental cost of industrial agriculture, many are turning back to this ancestral practice, seeking a more sustainable, wholesome way to eat. Urban foragers are even redefining what's considered edible, turning city parks and forgotten urban spaces into surprising sources of nutrition. In this rediscovery, foraging is more than just a culinary trend—it's a shared activity that can foster community ties, connecting you deeply with your food, your health, and the planet you inhabit.

These practices highlight an inherent respect for the land and a profound understanding that Mother Earth is not merely a provider but a partner to be honored and preserved. In its purest form, foraging is not about taking but participating in the grand circle of life. It celebrates a delicate balance of give and take. It fostered a love for the land and an intrinsic desire to protect it, principles that we, as modern foragers, should continue to uphold.

So, as you unravel the history of foraging, you must remember that each plant you identify and each berry you taste, echoes an ancient rhythm. A rhythm imprinted on our DNA and rooted in our shared history - a testament to our innate bond with the environment and a guide for our sustainable future.

Different Methods of Foraging

There are varied foraging strategies employed by human communities, each ingeniously adapted to their unique habitats. These time-tested methods reveal our ancestors' deep understanding of the world around them, painting a vivid portrait of the species' remarkable adaptability and resilience.

Let's start with the frost-kissed landscapes of the Arctic. Here, amidst towering icebergs and snow-covered expanses, the indigenous Inuit communities have perfected the art of foraging under the harshest of conditions. When the Arctic summer thaws the frost-locked landscapes, the Inuit people, attuned to the brief yet vibrant growth period, expertly forage for resilient Arctic plants. They seek out species such as crowberries, Arctic willow, and Labrador tea, leveraging generations of knowledge to identify and gather these plants without disturbing the fragile tundra ecosystem. This season allows the Inuits to stockpile essential nutrients for the harsh winter months when fresh food is scarce, demonstrating their intimate connection with the land, resilience, and resourcefulness.

Journey south, and you'll find yourself under the emerald canopy of the Amazon rainforest. The indigenous communities here are expert navigators of their realm, spotting fruits and nuts hidden in the lush foliage. Guided by generations of wisdom, they trace the intricate patterns of the forest, seeking out the ripe richness of acai berries, the high-protein punch of Brazil nuts, and the nourishing clusters of palm fruits.

In stark contrast, imagine the sun-drenched landscapes of Africa's deserts. Life here is a witness to endurance, with foraging skills tailored to navigate these arid plains. The pursuit of food is all about deciphering the sparse terrain for signs of life and water. With wisdom passed down generations, locals employ resourceful techniques to uncover edible plants concealed in the desert plains and trace elusive wildlife, providing a compelling demonstration of human adaptability.

These diverse practices across the globe reveal more than just survival strategies. They showcase the deep knowledge of the natural world held by indigenous communities, allowing them to thrive in their respective habitats.

Key Principles of Foraging

At the heart of foraging lie three pivotal principles. Once you practice keen observation, accurate identification, and ethical harvesting, you step into a legacy that extends back to our earliest ancestors, carrying it forward into a future where your survival may once again intertwine intimately with the wild.

Observation

You'll soon realize that simply seeing is vastly different from truly observing. Seeing can be passive—an act of receiving images that your eyes take in without your active participation. It's the surface level interaction you experience on a daily basis. Observing, on the other hand, is an active engagement with your environment. It is about connecting the dots, interpreting patterns, understanding relationships, and drawing conclusions.

When foraging, seeing might enable you to identify a patch of green grass in a sea of arid plains. But observing will allow you to distinguish between an edible plant and a potentially toxic look-alike, to identify a well-camouflaged mushroom hiding at the base of a tree, or to notice the signs that wild berries might be ripe for picking nearby.

As you hone your observational skills, you'll uncover nature's subtle cues, finding a trove of wild food that others might overlook. This is the beauty of foraging; it fosters a deep connection with nature, transforming a walk in the park or a hike in the woods into a culinary adventure. Through this, you are rekindling an age-old human instinct that has been dimmed by your modern lifestyle, and in the process, fosters a deep appreciation for the natural world.

Learning to truly observe rather than just see is important. But more than that, it's a perspective shift—a way to engage more deeply and meaningfully with the world around you. It's time to open your senses, embrace curiosity, and awaken your natural instinct to forage.

Identification

This principle requires a meticulous eye and an open mind. Some plants and fungi may seem alluringly edible but can harbor unseen dangers, while others, seemingly unremarkable, might hide a banquet of nutrition. Here's where reference books, field guides, and local expert advice become invaluable. Knowledge can be your greatest ally in the wild. However, accurate identification requires patience, practice, and a willingness to learn. It's a continuous process of studying, researching, and training that is honed with time and experience.

Each walk through the forest, hike in the mountains, or stroll through the park becomes an opportunity to learn. You start to notice the changes in flora as seasons transition, the unique characteristics of plants in different habitats, and the intricate ways in which species interact with each other. You'll find yourself constantly learning, and with each new discovery, the landscape will become a little less foreign.

Ethics

Finally, we come to Ethics, a principle that defines your relationship with the natural world. Foraging isn't merely a one-way transaction, it's a responsibility. Every mushroom plucked, every berry picked, should be done with the utmost respect for nature's bounty. Sustainable foraging practices include taking only what you need, leaving young plants to grow, and being mindful not to disturb the homes of animals. Equally important is the respect for legal boundaries and the rights of others—you should forage only where you have permission to do so.

The Importance of Foraging

Ever thought that a walk in the woods could be your pathway to improved well-being and a healthier planet? In this section, you will now look into how the simple act of foraging can become an essential part of your life, nurturing not only your body but also your mind and the beautiful Earth.

Lifeline in Survival Situations

Imagine you're stranded in a remote wilderness or navigating through the aftermath of a societal breakdown. Traditional food sources have run dry, and supermarket shelves are barren. It's here that the lifesaving importance of foraging leaps to the forefront.

In survival situations, foraging can be a key to unlocking the diverse buffet of nature. Foraged foods can also be nutritional goldmines packed with an array of essential vitamins, minerals, and antioxidants that are crucial for maintaining health in challenging conditions.

Beyond supplementing a nutritious diet, foraging can also offer a lifeline when food reserves are dwindling. When you incorporate foraged items into daily meals, you can stretch out your remaining food supplies. In times of uncertainty, this strategy can be a game-changer, making the difference between scarcity and sustainability.

Foraging Beyond Food

The world of foraging also extends beyond mere nutrition. When the conveniences of modern life are stripped away, nature's toolkit opens up. Medical supplies, shelter, and tools may become luxury items in survival situations. Yet, nature, through foraging, can provide.

Consider the soothing aloe vera, the calming lavender, or the healing plantain - these are nature's medicine cabinets that are easily accessible if you know where to look. Similarly, the wilderness abounds with materials for shelter construction or tool creation. A forager's discerning eye can turn a forest or a field into a haven of resources, easing survival hardships.

There's another often overlooked dimension to foraging - it's not just about the body but also the mind. In survival situations, stress and anxiety can run high. Here, foraging serves as a beacon of hope, offering a sense of purpose and accomplishment. It reminds you that you're not powerless and can take control of your circumstances. This sense of empowerment can fuel resilience, lift spirits, and enhance mental wellbeing amidst adversity.

Then there's the subtle yet profound connection with nature that foraging fosters. Even in the grimmest of survival situations, the act of foraging can spark a sense of wonder for your surroundings. This connection not only brings solace but also nurtures an appreciation for the natural world that can inspire sustainable practices, extending far beyond the immediate survival scenario.

Other Benefits of Foraging

Stepping beyond the basic idea of foraging as a survival tool, it also has other benefits and uses. From boosting mental well-being to fostering community spirit, the foraging journey goes far beyond the forest.

Physical Wellness

Foraging can affect your physical well-being positively. It encourages you to engage in gentle but effective exercise, like walking, bending, reaching, and even climbing, enhancing your overall fitness. Furthermore, wild foods are a veritable goldmine of nutrients. Rich in vitamins, minerals, antioxidants, and dietary fiber, they offer unique health benefits that are often superior to their cultivated counterparts.

Mental Health Boost

Foraging, as a hobby, also works wonders for mental health. It's therapeutic, grounding you in the present moment, just as mindfulness meditation does. A sense of peace comes from connecting with nature, from feeling the sun on your skin and hearing the rustle of leaves underfoot. This connection can lower stress levels, elevate mood, and improve overall emotional well-being. For example, studies have shown that spending time in green spaces reduces cortisol levels – the body's primary stress hormone.

Enhances Culinary Experiences

Ever tried a wild morel mushroom? Its complex, nutty flavor far surpasses that of any store-bought variety. Or what about the tart crunch of sea buckthorn berries? These vibrant orange gems, often foraged from coastal bushes, can turn a simple dish into an exotic taste sensation. Foraging can completely transform your culinary world, inviting you to explore a plethora of unique flavors, textures, and aromas.

Incorporating wild foods into your diet allows you to tap into the wisdom of your ancestors, bringing forgotten flavors back to modern plates. Plus, it sparks creativity in the kitchen as you experiment with unfamiliar ingredients, crafting meals that are as delightful to the taste buds as they nourish the body.

Fosters Sustainable Living and Foraging

In an era of growing environmental concern, foraging emerges as a sustainable alternative to conventional food procurement methods. Unlike large-scale farming, it doesn't require vast amounts of land, synthetic fertilizers, pesticides, or fossil fuels for machinery and transport.

As I've mentioned, foraging champions a "take what you need" ethos, urging you to harvest responsibly and ensuring that plant populations continue to thrive. This encourages biodiversity, supporting ecosystems by letting plants complete their life cycles, from flowering to seeding.

Moreover, it can also play a part in controlling invasive species. In many regions, invasive plants like garlic mustard or Japanese knotweed proliferate, threatening local biodiversity. Foragers can help keep these populations in check by harvesting them for consumption.

Encourages Community Building

Finally, foraging can serve as a potent community-building tool. When you share foraging tips, exchange recipes, or organize communal foraging trips, you can forge bonds of camaraderie. For instance, in urban settings, foraging groups often form to explore local parks or community gardens and brings a sense of togetherness and shared purpose.

Safety Precautions

I remember my first foraging trip, excitement bubbling over. Little did I know, there was more to it than just picking up what caught my eye. Foraging is a joy, yes, but it's also about ensuring your safety. Here are some tips I want you to keep in mind when foraging.

Dress Appropriately

Foraging, much like an adventure game in Mother Nature's arena, requires the right armor. Dressing for the occasion in long pants, long sleeves, and sturdy, closed-toe shoes is a must. This trusty outfit serves as your first line of defense against the wilderness' minor inconveniences, such as prickly nettles, pesky ticks, or the unforgiving sun. Let's not forget a hat either - not only to shield from the sun but also to fend off any possible falling objects.

The Forager's Toolkit

Next on the safety list is a toolkit fit for a foraging adventure. Navigating the outdoors requires more than just intuition; the items listed below are all critical additions to your equipment list.

- **Field Guide:** This is your go-to book or app that provides valuable information about local plants and fungi, including which are edible and which are not. An accurate, reliable guide can significantly improve your identification skills and keep you safe from harmful or toxic species.
- **Map or GPS Device:** Knowing where you are at all times is key to a safe foraging experience. A detailed map of the area or a reliable GPS device can help you track your location and ensure you don't get lost.
- **Compass:** Even in the age of technology, a traditional compass can come in handy, especially in areas with poor cell reception. It's an invaluable tool for navigation and orientation.

- **Multi-Tool:** This versatile tool can serve numerous functions, from cutting plant stems to opening cans or bottles. Look for one that includes a knife, scissors, a saw, and a bottle opener at the minimum.
- **Whistle:** A whistle can be a lifesaver in an emergency situation. Its loud sound can alert others to your location if you're lost or in trouble.
- **First Aid Kit:** Accidents can happen, so it's best to be prepared. Your kit should include bandages, antiseptic wipes, tweezers, medical tape, and any personal medication you might need.
- **Baskets:** Ideally, you should have a sturdy and roomy basket for carrying the fruits of your foraging efforts. Traditional woven baskets are a great option because they are lightweight, strong, and allow air circulation to keep your finds fresh. Some even prefer using backpacks with multiple compartments for different types of forage.
- **Gloves:** Protecting your hands from thorns, insects, or potentially irritating plants is important. A pair of durable gloves can provide this protection while still allowing the dexterity needed to forage effectively.

Bring Water

There's no doubt, foraging is a captivating adventure that can have us so engrossed, time seems just to melt away. But here's a piece of advice from one foraging friend to another - always bring a water bottle. As thrilling as the foraging journey is, it's equally taxing and can span long, unexpected hours. Thus, consider water a reliable partner in this grand escapade. It helps sustain your energy, sharpens your focus, and fends off fatigue and dizziness.

Now, you may ask, "Can't I just find water while I'm out there?" Absolutely! Nature often generously provides, but if you have the means, why not bring a guaranteed clean, safe supply with you? After all, natural sources may not always be readily available or entirely safe to consume. So, don't forget to quench your thirst as you quench your curiosity in the wilderness.

Develop Awareness

An experienced forager is always vigilant, keeping an eye out for potential hazards. Be it slippery terrains, falling trees, or potentially dangerous wildlife, your awareness can make all the difference. As an avid forager, here are some general reminders I want to impart to you when you are in nature.

- Slippery terrains, precipitous slopes, or muddy paths can transform a joyful forage into a risky venture, so make sure your steps are always measured and your balance steady.
- Keep an eye on the skies as well - falling trees or even loose branches can pose an unexpected danger, especially in windy conditions or in the aftermath of a storm. Remember, your safety always comes first.
- The wilderness is also home to a diverse range of wildlife. While spotting a deer or rabbit can add to the charm of your foraging expedition, encountering a bear, a snake, or even a nest of wasps is an entirely different story. Knowing the local wildlife and how to react in the presence of potentially dangerous animals is a crucial aspect of foraging safety.
- Also, while a field dotted with mushrooms or a thicket dense with plants might look like a forager's paradise, caution is key. High concentrations of certain plants or mushrooms could indicate the presence of toxic varieties. Therefore, your knowledge of local species and keen observation skills are vital.

Practice Caution

Rivers and streams can surge unexpectedly, cliff edges can be unstable, and marshy areas can be more treacherous than they appear. Nature is filled with surprises, both pleasant and challenging, so remain cautious and prepared as you immerse yourself in the foraging experience.

Choose Your Foraging Grounds Wisely

When embarking on your adventure, not all green spaces are safe spaces. Like an artist choosing the perfect canvas or a chef selecting the finest ingredients, a forager too must exercise discernment in choosing their foraging grounds. The backdrop for your hunt can dramatically influence not just the variety and abundance of forgeable goods but also their safety and quality.

Industrial areas, for instance, might seem unlikely spots for nature to flourish, and yet, you might be surprised to find clusters of plants or mushrooms thriving there. However, these unlikely foraging grounds come with a hidden danger. Over time, toxins from industrial waste or pollutants can leach into the soil and water, being absorbed by the very plants and mushrooms you might be tempted to harvest. The consequence? A plateful of contaminants rather than nutrients.

Similarly, water bodies like rivers or ponds look refreshing and pure, but it's important to consider their upstream. Are they flowing past factories or through agricultural land? If yes, there's a possibility they could be carrying harmful pollutants and pesticides. These substances, just like industrial waste, can accumulate in the plants and fungi around these water bodies. Consuming such contaminated forage can put your health at risk, a scenario far removed from the wholesome and healthful foraging experience many aspire to.

Areas that have been sprayed with pesticides should also be avoided. The very bugs these chemicals are meant to fend off might be pests to some, but they are a part of the intricate web of ecosystems. More importantly, those pesticides don't discriminate – they cling to plants and mushrooms just as readily as they do pests, making them unsafe to consume.

So, when you're lacing up your boots and readying your basket, remember to do a little homework first. Opt for spaces untouched by pollution, far from industrial sites, and away from potentially contaminated water bodies. Look for areas where nature is allowed to grow freely and safely. By doing so, you're not just ensuring a healthier and safer foraging experience, but you're also taking a stand for the kind of environment you want to interact with and support.

In later chapters, you'll delve deeper into these types of locations, exploring the specific challenges and opportunities each presents.

Keep Others in the Loop

You're about to embark on a exploration. But wait, there's one more step to take before you step into the wilderness - keeping others in the loop.

Imagine this: you're out there in the forest, enveloped by the rustling leaves, the murmuring wind, the whispering grass. It's just you and the vast expanse of nature. But what if you stumble upon an unforeseen situation? A twisted ankle on a rocky path, a sudden storm drenching the trails, or, albeit rarely, an unexpected encounter with local wildlife. These are instances when the outside world needs to know you're out there.

So, always inform a friend, a family member, or even a neighbor about your foraging plans before setting off. Share your intended location, your planned route, and, importantly, your estimated time of return. Keep them posted if you decide to extend your trip or change your location.

Consider it as leaving breadcrumbs in the digital world - a trail that leads back to you when needed. This way, in the event of any unexpected circumstances, help would know where to find you. Remember, it's not just about your safety but also about the peace of mind for those who care about you.

Being connected to others while engaging in such a solitary and immersive activity might seem counterintuitive at first. Yet, it's this very connection that wraps your adventure in an added layer of safety, making your foraging experience not only exciting but also reassuringly secure.

Chapter 2
Plant Identification Skills

One of the most rewarding experiences of foraging is the thrill of discovery. To walk in nature's pantry and spot that plump berry or a patch of wild garlic, your senses fill with excitement and gratitude. But for those unfamiliar, the landscape can appear confusing, even intimidating, filled with a vast array of green leaves, towering trees, and tiny flowers. The key to unlocking this green maze, and making foraging a safe and enjoyable endeavor, lies in mastering plant identification skills.

Plant identification is the primary skill that you must learn. It separates a dangerous guessing game from a wholesome gathering of nature's bounty. Developing the ability to identify plants is not always an easy task, especially when many plants look similar, and some are edible while others are not. I'll talk about why it's so important to know plants, the challenges you might face, and some helpful strategies for overcoming them. This chapter will also guide you through the steps to build this essential skill from the ground up, suitable for both the urban park and the wilderness, ensuring you can forage confidently and securely.

Importance

Plant identification is not just about knowing what's what—it's about your safety. You wouldn't blindly pick a mushroom from a forest floor and eat it, would you? The same goes for any plant. Accurate identification ensures you don't mistake a harmful plant for an edible one. Think of hemlock and wild carrot: the former, deadly; the latter, harmless and quite tasty. They are strikingly similar in appearance but dramatically different in effect. Learning to differentiate them could be lifesaving.

By also knowing what to look for, you can enjoy fresh, organic food throughout the year, straight from nature's pantry. To illustrate, if you are familiar with seasonal plants then you will not look for elderberries in spring because they are a summer and autumn fruit. This knowledge not only helps you to save time and effort but also to plan your foraging trips more effectively.

Plant identification also helps you forage responsibly, ensuring the survival and growth of plant populations. You wouldn't want to strip a plant clean of its fruits, leaving nothing for the wildlife that depends on it, would you? Let's take berries, for instance. It might be tempting to gather all the juicy blackberries from a bush, but remember that you're not the only one who relishes these fruits. Birds, insects, small mammals, and even other plants depend on those berries for nourishment and propagation. Leaving some berries behind means supporting a healthy ecosystem where all life forms can thrive.

With plant identification skills in your arsenal, you open the door to an incredible variety of tastes, textures, and nutritional benefits. Wild plants, often dismissed as weeds, are packed with nutrients that far surpass those found in common store-bought vegetables. Take dandelion, for example. This unassuming plant, often weeded from gardens, is a nutritional powerhouse, rich in vitamins A, C, K, and E, and minerals like iron and calcium. Once you know how to identify it, you've found yourself a free, nutritious, and easily available food source.

By recognizing the plants growing around you, you gain insight into their roles within the wider ecosystem. You'll no longer perceive the change of seasons as just a shift in weather patterns, but as a transformative period for plant life too. This increased awareness gives you a new perspective on the natural world, deepening your connection to and appreciation for it. Plant identification can contribute to your overall awareness and understanding of the natural world.

For children, this can be particularly impactful. Once they learn to identify plants, they can foster an early appreciation for nature, nurturing a generation of environmental stewards. For instance, a child knowing how to identify an oak tree could lead to understanding its importance as a home for countless birds, insects, and mammals, instilling respect for these ecological interactions.

Challenges of Identifying Plants

Picture over 300,000 plant species on the planet, each with their unique traits and life cycle. Now, imagine trying to pick out the ones that are not only edible but palatable and nutritious as well. The vast kaleidoscope of plant species presents a significant challenge to those new to foraging. It's a bit like finding the needle in a haystack. In fact, many plants that are tantalizingly similar to those you can eat can be harmful or even deadly. Take, for instance, the deadly nightshade, a spitting image of the innocent blueberry, a case of mistaken identity that could lead to a dire outcome. Also, each plant changes as it grows, and each growth stage could look different, which can make it tricky to identify.

The challenge is not only in finding edible plants but also in finding reliable information about them. While there is no shortage of guidebooks and online resources, their accuracy is a gamble. What's more, not all plants are ubiquitous; some prefer the warmer south, others the chilly north. Thus, an understanding of your local flora becomes your compass in this plant labyrinth.

The urban sprawl and land development, voracious as they are, have gobbled up much of natural habitats, making the quest for edible plants an adventure in itself. Not to mention the pollution and pesticides that pervade the environments, tainting the very plants you seek. It is not enough to find an edible plant; you must find one that has not dined on harmful chemicals. This means understanding the land around you, its history, its usage, and its health.

And then, of course, there's the hurdle of hands-on experience. Reading about plants and their characteristics is one thing. Seeing them in person, touching their leaves, smelling their flowers—that's a whole other ball game. Many details can be lost between the pages of a book and the canvas of nature. To bridge this gap, time and practice are your best allies. Workshops, outdoor courses, and walks with seasoned foragers can pave your way to becoming a confident plant identifier.

Societal biases, too, sometimes sneak in and may shape your perception of what's edible and what's not. Cultural leanings have sculpted dietary preferences over the ages, often blinding you to the nutritional treasures lurking in your backyard. In many industrialized nations, the idea of foraging for food might seem primitive or unnecessary, given the convenience of supermarkets. Breaking away from these biases opens up a new world of culinary possibilities, enriching your diet and foraging experience.

Seasonality, the final hurdle in your foraging journey, dictates the availability of plants. The earth's rhythm plays out in the life cycles of plants, making some available only at specific times of the year. Thus, a successful forager is not only a plant identifier but also a seasonal strategist, aware of the optimal harvest times and the necessary plan Bs when a favored plant is out of season.

Mastering Plant Identification

Undoubtedly, the path to mastering plant identification is lined with challenges. But these are far from insurmountable. With reliable guidebooks, apps, and, most importantly, practical hands-on experience, you can become adept at identifying plants. Join a local foraging group, take part in plant identification workshops, or even get a mentor. Aside from these, understanding plant families can be a game-changer in your foraging journey. Just like how knowing someone's family can provide insights into their characteristics, learning about plant families can help you predict the properties of plants you're not yet familiar with.

Different Plant Families

Knowing different plant families is a fundamental way of organizing and identifying plants in the wild. This is because the flower's appearance, leaf structure, and other characteristics can prove to be a very helpful guide in your foraging endeavors. Just like you wouldn't expect to find oranges growing on an apple tree, certain features, especially the flower's appearance, can give you clues about a plant's edibility, toxicity, and uses.

For instance, it's not always obvious what a plant is, especially if the edible part is hidden underground, like potatoes. If you know that potatoes belong to the Solanaceae family and recognize their flowers, you might recognize these wild potatoes or related edible species that are otherwise easy to miss and add them to your foraged food.

Asteraceae (Daisy) Family

The Asteraceae or Daisy family is known for its unique flowers. These plants produce what's known as a 'composite' flower head – a structure that looks like one large flower but is actually made up of many small ones. Each 'petal' you see around the outside of a sunflower or daisy is, in fact, a whole individual flower, or 'ray floret'. The center of these composite flower heads is packed with more tiny flowers, or 'disc florets'.

Another key characteristic is their leaves, which are generally simple and alternate (they are not paired on the stem and don't have a complex structure). However, their shapes and sizes can vary significantly from one species to another. For example, a dandelion has long, thin leaves that are jagged along the edges, while sunflower leaves are broad and heart-shaped.

These two are the most common species of this family. Dandelions are entirely edible - from their bright yellow flower heads to their long taproot. The young leaves can be tossed into a salad, the flowers can be used to make a sweet wine or tea, and the roots can be roasted and ground to make a caffeine-free coffee substitute.

Similarly, sunflowers, are a well-known source of edible seeds. These seeds can be eaten raw or roasted for a nuttier flavor. Sunflower seeds are often used in baking or to make sunflower butter, a tasty alternative to peanut butter.

The Fabaceae (Pea) Family

Fabaceae or Pea family members are recognized by their distinct flowers and leaves. The flowers often have a unique structure - a large petal on top (the banner), two side petals (the wings), and two bottom petals fused together (the keel). This arrangement somewhat resembles a butterfly and is thus called 'papilionaceous'. Pea and clover flowers are typical examples of this.

The leaves in the Fabaceae family are often compound (made up of several leaflets) and arranged alternately on the stem. The leaf edges are usually smooth. Additionally, many members of this family have tendrils for climbing and often produce their seeds in pods.

Plants of this family are power-packed sources of nutrition. For example, Chickpeas, lentils, and soybeans are rich in protein and form a dietary staple in many cultures. Chickpeas can be cooked and eaten on their own, ground into flour, or made into hummus, a popular Middle Eastern dip.

The green peas that people commonly consume are immature seeds of a plant from the Fabaceae family. They can be eaten raw, boiled, or steamed and added to a variety of dishes for their sweet flavor and vibrant color.

Lamiaceae (Mint) Family

Plants in the Lamiaceae or Mint family are relatively easy to identify. They typically have square stems and opposite leaves – a unique combination in plants. The leaves are generally simple, without leaflets, and usually have serrated edges.

The flowers are often brightly colored and come in various shapes, but many have a distinctive 'lipped' appearance, almost like a tiny open mouth. Additionally, many plants in this family, like mint, basil, or lavender, have a strong scent when their leaves are crushed.

Rosaceae (Rose) Family

The Rosaceae or Rose family is known for its notable members: apples, strawberries, cherries, and raspberries, among others. The flowers usually have five petals and numerous stamens, creating a stunning floral display. Leaves are often alternately arranged, and most have a serrated edge.

The fruits from the Rosaceae family can be easily recognized. For instance, wild strawberries are small, heart-shaped fruits, red when ripe, with tiny seeds on the surface. Apples, though larger, also have seeds on the inside of a fleshy fruit. Not all fruits from the Rose family are edible, and some may even be toxic, so make sure to properly identify them before consumption.

Solanaceae (Nightshade) Family

The Solanaceae or Nightshade family includes a diverse range of plants, from tasty tomatoes and hearty potatoes to potentially deadly belladonna. These plants often have alternate leaves, which can vary from simple to pinnately compound. Their flowers typically have five petals and are fused together into a tube or bell shape.

While the edible members of this family, like tomatoes and eggplants, are well known, caution must be exercised with wild members of this family. For example, black nightshade berries may look appealing but can be toxic.

Brassicaceae (Mustard) Family

The Brassicaceae or Mustard family is easily identified thanks to their distinct flowers. Their four petals are often arranged in a cross shape, hence the family's old name, Cruciferae, meaning 'cross-bearing'. The leaves of these plants are alternate and often lobed.

Many familiar vegetables hail from this family, including cabbage, broccoli, and kale. Wild mustards can be identified by their bright yellow or white cross-shaped flowers and the spicy, peppery taste of their leaves and seeds.

Tips to Avoid Poisonous Plants

The beauty of nature can sometimes mask hidden dangers. Among these are poisonous plants, whose ingestion can lead to severe health problems. To help you set them apart from edible plants, here are some tips you can follow to ensure safety.

Avoid the Temptation of Unknown Berries

While out in the wild, the sight of luscious, colorful berries can be tantalizing. However, caution is crucial as not all berries are safe for consumption. One of the most notorious examples is the red, tempting berry of the yew tree. These berries, though enjoyed by birds, are deadly to humans if consumed. Many other toxic berries can lure the unsuspecting forager with their vibrant hues. The deadly nightshade, for instance, produces glossy black berries that can be easily mistaken for the harmless blackberry. So, when you come across unknown berries, resist the urge to taste them unless you can identify them with absolute certainty.

Stay Clear of Unknown Leaves and Stems

Emerald-green patches of plants might look inviting and brimming with potential food sources. However, certain leaves and stems can spell trouble. Plants such as poison ivy, poison oak, and poison sumac are infamous for the skin irritation and rashes they cause upon contact. To identify them, Poison ivy typically grows leaves in three clusters with a shiny or waxy appearance. On the other hand, poison oak also grows in sets of three leaves but may sometimes sport clusters of five or seven, with leaves resembling those of an oak tree. While poison sumac stands out with 7 to 13 leaves on a branch, with each leaf having a smooth edge. Awareness of these characteristics can help you avoid unpleasant encounters with these plants.

Be Wary of Roots and Tubers

The world beneath the soil - the domain of roots and tubers - can be a treasure trove of nutrients. However, not all that glitter is gold. Some plants harbor toxic roots, while their leaves and fruits may be perfectly safe to eat. Additionally, some plants have roots that are edible but need appropriate preparation to neutralize their harmful components. The cassava is a perfect example of this, with its roots being rich in cyanogenic glycosides, a toxin that can convert to cyanide in the body. However, by peeling and cooking the cassava thoroughly, this toxin can be deactivated, rendering the root safe to eat.

Avoid Plants with Bitter Taste

Nature often communicates through flavors, and bitterness is one of its ways of saying 'beware'. Plants have evolved to develop bitter tastes to deter animals from consuming them, and humans have evolved to find such flavors unappetizing. Many poisonous plants, such as the infamous hemlock and certain parts of the elderberry plant, leave a bitter taste in the mouth, which should serve as a red flag during foraging.

Watch Out for Milky or Discolored Sap

Several toxic plants secrete a milky or discolored sap when they're cut or broken. Examples of such plants include milkweed and poisonwood. This sap can cause severe skin irritation and may lead to more severe reactions in some individuals. Therefore, when you come across a plant oozing such sap, it's best to keep your distance

Never Rush to Eat

Patience is a virtue, especially when it comes to foraging. Don't rush to eat something you've foraged. Instead, take your time to inspect the plant. Is it familiar? Can you confidently identify it? If not, it's best to leave it be.

Learn from Experienced Foragers

There's no substitute for experience. Join a local foraging group, if possible. Learning from those who have years of experience foraging can be incredibly beneficial. They can provide first-hand knowledge about which plants to avoid and those that are safe to consume.

Universal Edibility Test

Safe foraging hinges on knowledge, caution, and respect for nature's power. You can avoid the dangers of poisonous plants by equipping yourself with the right knowledge, staying alert, and double-checking everything before you consume it. And when in doubt, always remember the golden rule of foraging: if you're not sure what it is, don't eat it. Yet, in desperate situations, you can use the 'Universal Edibility Test' if you're unsure about a plant but are considering eating it. Here's the step-by-step process.

1. **Separate the Plant Components.** Each part of the plant - the leaves, stems, roots, buds, flowers, or fruit - may have different properties. Some plants have parts that are edible, while others are not. For instance, the leaves of the rhubarb plant are toxic, whereas the stalks can be safely consumed. Thus, it is highly advisable to separate and test each part of the plant independently.
2. **Inspect the Plant.** Before you proceed with the rest of the test, take a careful look at each part of the plant. Does it emit a strong or unpleasant odor when crushed? If yes, it's likely not safe to eat. Do the leaves have a shiny surface or come in groups of three? These are common characteristics of poisonous plants like poison ivy and poison oak. Plants with thorns, fine hairs, or spines are also typically unsafe to eat.

3. **Contact Test.** In this step, you're testing for dermal reactions. By crushing part of the plant and rubbing it onto a sensitive part of your skin, like the inside of your wrist or elbow, you can check for immediate allergic reactions. Look out for signs like redness, a rash, itching, or burning. If any of these symptoms appear, you can conclude that the plant is unsafe to consume.
4. **Prepare the Plant.** If the plant part doesn't cause any skin reactions, prepare it as you would for eating. This could be peeling it, boiling it, or grinding it, depending on what's feasible in your situation. If you're boiling the plant part, remember to keep the used water separate and not consume it, as it could contain leached toxins.
5. **Lip Test.** Touch a small portion of the prepared plant part to your outer lip. Just like the contact test for your skin, this tests for any adverse reactions. Pay close attention to any sensations of burning, itching, or numbness. If you experience any of these reactions, it's a clear sign that the plant is unsafe to eat.
6. **Tongue Test.** If there are no adverse reactions from the lip test, you can proceed to place the plant part on your tongue. Remember not to swallow it at this stage. Any signs of discomfort, such as a burning sensation or numbness, indicate that the plant part should not be consumed.
7. **Chew, But Do Not Swallow.** Chewing allows the plant's juices to come into contact with your mouth and throat. This can reveal potential irritants or toxins that might not have been detected in the previous steps. Keep the chewed plant in your mouth for 15 minutes but avoid swallowing. Spit it out immediately if you feel any discomfort.
8. **Swallow a Small Portion.** If the plant part doesn't cause any reactions when chewed, you can now swallow a small piece. The stomach and intestines are in different environments and can react differently to potential toxins. Again, this is a cautious step in the testing process.

9. **Wait for 24 Hours.** This is perhaps the most important part of the test. Some plant toxins take time to manifest symptoms, and these may not be immediately apparent. During this waiting period, do not eat anything else that could potentially confuse the results. Pay close attention to any signs of discomfort, such as nausea, diarrhea, cramps, or other forms of distress.
10. **Eat a Small Amount.** If you've come this far without any negative reactions, it's likely that the plant part is safe to eat. However, you should still proceed with caution. Start by consuming a small amount of the plant and continue to monitor your body for any delayed reactions.

Each of these steps is designed to protect you from potential harm. While it may seem like a slow process, remember that safety is paramount when foraging and testing unknown plants. This test should only be used as a last resort, with the understanding that it isn't foolproof. Your best defense is knowledge, so whenever possible, study the plants in your area and use reliable resources to help identify them.

Seasonal Foraging

Nature doesn't stand still - it has seasons, at least for most parts of the world. This is intrinsically tied to the life cycles of plants and shapes the opportunities for foraging throughout the year.

If you've ever admired the beauty of cherry blossom in spring, tasted the sweetness of a freshly picked strawberry in summer, crunched on a crisp apple in fall, or savored the earthiness of a winter root vegetable, then you've already engaged in a form of seasonal awareness. Seasonal foraging is about taking this awareness a step further and understanding how nature's cycles provide a diverse menu of wild edibles all year round. From the first green shoots of spring to the hardy survivors of winter, each season has its own unique foraging opportunities.

Spring

Spring is a time of renewal when nature wakes up from its winter sleep, and everything seems to spring to life almost overnight. The first edible plants to appear as the ground warms are often green shoots, tender leaves, and early flowers.

- **Wild Greens**: Fresh leaves of plants like dandelions, chickweed, and nettles make for a nutritious, delicious salad or cooked green. *Foraging tip:* pick the young, tender leaves—they're more delicate in flavor and texture.
- **Flowering Trees**: Spring is also the season for flowering trees. The blossoms of apple, cherry, and hawthorn trees are not only beautiful but also edible. They can be used to infuse drinks, make jellies, or simply eat fresh off the tree.

Summer

As we move into summer, the plant life continues to thrive. This is a period of great productivity and maturity for many plants. They now focus on flowering and producing fruits and seeds, their means of reproduction. The result is a bounty of berries, fruits, and herbs ripe for the summer forager's picking.

- **Berries**: Wild berries are a summer foraging favorite. From strawberries to raspberries, blackberries to blueberries, these delicious fruits are found in fields, forests, and even along roadsides. However, berry foraging comes with a warning: some berries are toxic, and a few look very similar to their edible counterparts. Always be sure of your identification before eating any wild berries.
- **Herbs**: Summer is also an ideal time to collect wild herbs. Plants like wild mint, sage, and rosemary are in full bloom, making it an ideal time to harvest them for both culinary and medicinal uses.

Autumn

Autumn signals the onset of cooler days and shorter daylight hours. Many plants respond by starting to wind down their above-ground activity. However, this is the season when trees drop their nuts, and many plants release their seeds—providing another rich source of foraged food.

- **Nuts:** Autumn is the time for nuts. Hazelnuts, walnuts, and acorns are just a few of the wild nuts you can forage. Collect them straight from the ground where they've fallen, then roast or grind them for a variety of uses.
- **Seeds:** Many plants go to seed in the autumn, providing a great opportunity for foraging. For example, sunflower seeds and pumpkin seeds can be gathered, cleaned, and roasted for a nutritious snack.

Winter

When winter rolls around, the landscape may seem barren and lifeless, but life is still there, just in a more subtle form. Many plants have retreated underground, storing energy in their roots. These roots, along with the hardy winter greens that can withstand the cold, provide foraging opportunities even in the bleakest months.

- **Roots:** Many plants store nutrients in their roots over the winter, making this the perfect time for root foraging. Plants like burdock and dandelion have roots that can be harvested in winter for a hearty addition to soups and stews.
- **Barks and Twigs:** Winter is also a good time to forage for tree barks and twigs. Pine bark, for instance, can be steeped into a vitamin C-rich tea, while willow twigs contain salicin, a compound similar to aspirin.

Building Your Foraging Calendar

While this guide provides a broad overview, the specific timing and availability of plants will depend on your local climate and ecosystems. Therefore, a crucial part of seasonal foraging is learning the rhythms of your own local nature.

Start by regularly walking in the same natural spaces throughout the year. Notice the cycles of plants: when they first sprout, when they flower, when they bear fruit, and when they die back. Over time, you'll start to develop your foraging calendar, a personalized guide to what's available in your area and when.

Activity: Plant Bingo

One enjoyable way to enhance your knowledge of plant foraging is through a game I like to call "Plant Bingo." This exercise makes learning about different plants interactive and entertaining.

Here's how you can set up and play:

1. Create Your Bingo Cards
   First, you'll need to create your plant bingo cards. Research the common plants in your area, especially the edible ones, and choose the 24 that you'd like to find. Sketch or print pictures of each plant, making sure to include its leaves, flowers, or fruits, as these are often key identifying features. Arrange these images randomly on a 5x5 grid, leaving the central square as a "free space."
2. Prepare for Your Foraging Adventure
   Before you go out, make sure you're equipped with your plant bingo card, a pencil to mark off the plants you find, and a good local plant identification guidebook or a reliable plant identification app. Remember to dress appropriately

for the weather and wear good walking shoes. A small basket or bag might also come in handy for collecting small samples for closer inspection.
3. Let the Game Begin!
Now you're ready for your foraging adventure. As you walk, keep your eyes open for any plants that match those on your bingo card. When you spot one, mark it off. If you're unsure about a plant, use your guidebook or app to help with identification.
4. Get a Bingo
The goal of the game is to get five plants in a row, column, or diagonal - just like traditional bingo. But who's to say you can't aim for a "full house" and find every plant on your card?

Playing Plant Bingo not only deepens your understanding of different plants, but it also hones your observation skills, sharpens your plant identification abilities, and, most importantly, adds an element of fun to your foraging journeys. You can play it alone or with friends and family. You could even turn it into a friendly competition to see who can get bingo first!

Chapter 3
Medicinal Plant Foraging

Suppose you're out in the wilderness, far from civilization, when disaster strikes. Maybe it's an unexpected twist of weather, or perhaps it's a societal hiccup that cascades into full-blown chaos. Now, let's throw a spanner in the works. Traditional medical resources have dried up, pharmacies are ghost towns, and hospitals - those citadels of modern healthcare - are either non-existent or teetering on the brink of collapse. Daunting, isn't it? Now, what if I told you that you could not only survive but thrive in such a situation? All by harnessing the healing powers hiding in plain sight in nature's verdant pharmacy.

Think of yourself as an explorer, scanning the wilderness with an enlightened gaze. You see a patch of aloe vera and instantly recognize it as a natural burn salve. You stumble upon a field of chamomile and lavender, not just aromatic herbs but powerful relaxants that can lull you into a soothing sleep or melt away anxiety. This is the incredible potential you unlock when you master foraging for medicinal plants. It all starts with understanding the diverse uses of medicinal plants, identifying them in the wilderness, and being able to prepare them.

Uses of Medicinal Plants

Medicinal plants offer an exciting realm of healing possibilities, a natural pharmacy gifted by Mother Nature. Across different cultures and history, they've been revered for their contribution to health and wellness is immense, from curing chronic ailments to being an emergency savior in survival scenarios. This section explores the powerful potential of medicinal plants, offering a glimpse into their varied uses.

Healing and Wellness

Healing is a broad term that encompasses an array of health concerns. It can range from alleviating mild conditions, like headaches or digestive issues, to combating severe illnesses. Medicinal plants play a critical role in this healing process. They're packed with a myriad of natural compounds, each having specific therapeutic effects that contribute to overall well-being.

For instance, certain plants have been used traditionally to alleviate headaches. They do this by reducing inflammation, dilating blood vessels, and relieving tension. In a similar vein, some plants can provide relief from digestive discomfort. They can soothe the gut, reduce bloating, and help maintain healthy gut flora, leading to improved digestion.

Medicinal plants have also been traditionally used to aid the healing process of various injuries, from minor scratches and burns to significant wounds. Certain plants are known to help reduce inflammation and swelling, which can be particularly beneficial in the case of sprains or strains. They work by decreasing the body's inflammatory response, providing relief from pain and discomfort. They can also help promote wound healing through the process of skin regeneration. This reduces the chances of infection, and even minimize scarring.

In addition to their healing properties, these plants can be incorporated into your daily life for general health maintenance and disease prevention. Some can aid in promoting a good night's sleep, helping those who suffer from insomnia. Others can be effective stress relievers, helping to calm the mind and body and providing relief from anxiety and stress-related issues.

Adding them into your daily diet can also boost your immunity. They are loaded with beneficial compounds that strengthen the body's natural defenses, making you less prone to illnesses. Moreover, some plants can contribute to maintaining good skin health. They can help cleanse the skin, fight against acne, and even contribute to a youthful and radiant complexion.

Survival

In the wilderness, medicinal plants can be lifesavers. These green gems can provide essential nutrients, ward off potential illnesses, and even act as a food source.

Some have natural antibiotic properties that can help keep potential infections at bay. They can also serve as a first-aid solution for minor cuts and wounds, helping in the process of wound cleaning and preventing further complications.

Lastly, these plants are nutritionally rich and can be consumed in survival scenarios. They can provide essential vitamins and minerals, helping the body maintain its energy levels and keeping starvation at bay.

Common Medicinal Plants

Long before the birth of modern medicine, our ancestors turned to the natural world for remedies to their ailments. From the green forests of the ancient Celts to the riverbanks of early Egyptian civilizations, the wisdom of using medicinal plants has been passed down through generations. These botanical treasures offered a way to soothe a throbbing headache, heal a stubborn wound, or calm a restless mind, creating the foundation for many of today's pharmaceutical marvels.

Aloe Vera

Native to the arid landscapes of Africa, the Aloe Vera is a succulent plant that can grow up to 1-2 feet in height. It exhibits a rosette of leaves that sprawl out from a central base. Each leaf is a thick, fleshy paddle and contains a gel-like substance that has been used for centuries to treat a variety of skin ailments, including burns, cuts, and rashes. In addition, it's often used in skin care products for its moisturizing and anti-aging benefits, and some studies suggest that when ingested, aloe vera may aid digestion and boost the immune system.

Their color can range from bright green to a gray-green hue, sometimes showcasing white freckles on the upper and lower stem surfaces. The leaves' margins have tiny white teeth, sharp to the touch, and taper into a mucronate or pointed tip. The plant occasionally blooms in the summer, pushing up a tall, slender stalk from the center. This stalk boasts a spire of yellow, tubular flowers that are both beautiful and fragrant.

Chamomile

Chamomile comes in many species, but the German Chamomile (Matricaria recutita) and Roman Chamomile (Chamaemelum nobile) are most commonly used for medicinal purposes. Both species are small, creeping plants, often not exceeding a foot in height. They have finely dissected, feather-like leaves, giving them an almost fern-like appearance. The flowers, appearing from early to midsummer, are the most characteristic feature of chamomile. They are small, daisy-like, with bright yellow disc florets at the center and white ray florets encircling them.

The flowers are often dried and used in teas to help promote sleep and relaxation. It can also be used to soothe stomach aches, reduce inflammation, and treat skin conditions. Chamomile also has antiseptic properties, and it's often found in topical skin treatments to accelerate healing and reduce inflammation.

Mint

Belonging to the Mentha genus, mint is a fast-growing, invasive plant. It's widely used in cooking and beverages for its refreshing flavor. Mint is also known for its digestive benefits, often consumed as a tea to soothe an upset stomach or aid digestion. Furthermore, it's commonly used in oral hygiene products like toothpaste and mouthwash due to its fresh aroma and antibacterial properties.

To identify it, mint features a square-shaped stem, a unique characteristic of plants in the Lamiaceae family. The leaves are arranged in opposite pairs, each leaf oval to lanceolate in shape, and edges coarsely serrated. Depending on the species, the color of leaves can vary from bright green to purplish, even silver. Mint plants bloom small, delicate flowers from mid to late summer, clustered in the leaf axils or at the stem tips. The flowers can be white, pink, or purple, with four distinct lobes.

Echinacea

Echinacea, or purple coneflower, is a sturdy, perennial plant native to North America. It can grow up to 1-2 feet tall, displaying large, showy flowers. The individual leaves are lance-shaped, with a rough texture, and have a rich green hue. The flowers, blooming from early to late summer, have a unique appearance. They consist of a central, spiky cone that's dark orange or brown, surrounded by drooping, petal-like ray florets. These florets are typically vibrant purple-pink, giving the plant its common name.

Echinacea is well-known for its immune-boosting properties. The roots and aerial parts of the plant are often used in herbal supplements to fight infections, especially common colds and other respiratory infections. It also has anti-inflammatory properties and can be used topically to help heal wounds, burns, and other skin problems.

Plantain

Plantain (Plantago major) is a low-growing herb that's often mistaken for a weed. Despite its weed-like appearance, plantain is a medicinal powerhouse. It's been used for centuries to soothe and heal wounds, burns, and skin inflammations. Chewing fresh plantain leaves and applying them to the skin can provide quick relief for insect bites. Its leaves can also be brewed into a tea that soothes respiratory problems and aids digestion.

It exhibits rosettes of leaves radiating from a central point at ground level. Each leaf is oval, thick, and fibrous, with parallel veins running from the base to the tip. In the summer, the plant sends up a tall, leafless stalk, sometimes up to 10 inches high. These flower stalks bear tiny, dense clusters of white flowers, which later develop into seed pods.

Lavender

Lavender (Lavandula) is a small, aromatic shrub known for its purple or violet flowers. It can reach up to 2 feet in height, featuring numerous branches of silvery-green, narrow, linear leaves. The flowers bloom on long, slender, spike-like stems from late spring to early autumn. Each flower spike is a collection of small, tubular blossoms ranging from pale lilac to deep purple, depending on the species.

Its flowers have a characteristic smell that makes it easily identifiable. Lavender is cherished for its soothing fragrance and is often used in aromatherapy to reduce anxiety and promote relaxation.

It is commonly used in potpourri, sachets, and cosmetics. Lavender oil, extracted from the flowers, is used in a variety of skincare and bath products. Additionally, lavender can be used in culinary applications, from flavoring baked goods and desserts to crafting herbed oils and vinegars.

Ways to Prepare and Use Medicinal Plants

With increasing interest in self-sustainability and natural health, many are turning back to the ancient wisdom of medicinal preparation methods. Even with zero knowledge about foraging or medicine, you can learn and appreciate the diverse range of preparation methods, transforming foraged plants into effective remedies.

Herbal Infusions

Herbal infusions are one of the simplest and most common methods of medicinal preparation. Essentially, this involves steeping plant material in a hot liquid, usually water, to extract the beneficial components. Think of it as making tea. The difference is that, for medicinal purposes, the steeping process is generally longer, typically about 15-30 minutes.

To illustrate, imagine making chamomile tea. Fresh or dried chamomile flowers are placed in a cup, boiling water is poured over, and the mixture is covered and left to steep. After the infusion time, the flowers are strained out, resulting in a warm, calming drink used for centuries to soothe anxiety and aid sleep.

Tinctures

Tinctures are another popular medicinal preparation method. They involve soaking plant material in alcohol or vinegar to extract their active medicinal properties, creating a concentrated liquid. Tinctures have a long shelf life, making them a practical choice for storing medicinal herbs.

A common plant used for this is echinacea which is renowned for its immune-boosting properties. To create an echinacea tincture, you'd fill a glass jar with chopped fresh echinacea root, leaves, and flowers, cover them with high-proof alcohol, and let it sit for about six weeks. After straining, you're left with a potent liquid that can be taken in small doses at the first sign of a cold.

Salves and Balms

Salves and balms are topical treatments that deliver medicinal plant benefits directly to the skin. They involve infusing plant material in oil, straining, and then combining the oil with beeswax to create a solid, shelf-stable product.

If you want to make this, you may use calendula due to its exceptional skin-healing properties. Calendula flowers are infused in carrier oil like olive or coconut for a few weeks. After straining, the oil is gently heated with beeswax until it melts. Once cooled, you have a natural salve ideal for minor cuts, burns, or dry skin.

Syrups

Herbal syrups are delightful preparations that combine medicinal plants, water, and a sweetener such as honey or sugar. They are often used for soothing sore throats or coughs and can make the medicine more palatable for children.

A classic example is elderberry syrup. To prepare, elderberries are simmered in water, then strained. The liquid is combined with honey, resulting in a syrup that's delicious and packed with immune-boosting properties.

Exercise: Creating Your Own Herbal Infusion

For this exercise, you're going to create your very own herbal infusion. You'll gain firsthand experience of medicinal preparation and you'll come to appreciate the wonderful benefits medicinal plants have to offer. You will use Chamomile as it's widely available and known for its calming properties. But if you have another preference or if Chamomile isn't suitable for you, feel free to choose another herb.

Materials Needed:

- Fresh or dried chamomile flowers (or an herb of your choice)
- A cup
- Boiling water
- A strainer
- A timer

Steps:

1. **Observe the Plant.** Begin by taking a moment to look at your chamomile. Observe the beautiful petals and the pleasant aroma. Think about how this simple plant has potent medicinal properties. How does it make you feel?
2. **Start the Infusion.** Place about one tablespoon of chamomile flowers in your cup and fill it with boiling water.
3. **Steep.** Let the chamomile steep in the hot water. Set your timer for 15-30 minutes. During this time, try to clear your mind. Perhaps use this waiting time for a bit of mindfulness or meditation.
4. **Strain and Sip.** When the timer goes off, strain the chamomile flowers out of the water. The liquid left is your chamomile tea, or more technically, your chamomile infusion.

5. **Enjoy.** Take a moment to enjoy the calming aroma before taking your first sip. As you sip, close your eyes and focus on the taste. Can you identify any specific notes or flavors? Notice how your body reacts. Do you feel more relaxed or calm?
6. **Reflect.** After finishing your infusion, take a few minutes to reflect on the experience. What did you enjoy about the process? How do you feel now, compared to before you drank the infusion? Write down your thoughts in a journal.

This exercise offers a simple but effective way to experience the power of medicinal plants. Remember, appreciating medicinal plants is not just about their health benefits; it's about forming a deeper connection with nature and learning to enjoy the simple things in life. As you savor your homemade infusion, you're not just consuming a drink; you're participating in an ancient tradition of using plants as medicine.

Chapter 4
Protein-Rich Foraging

Now, you might be wondering, "Can I really find protein in the wild only by?" The answer is a resounding yes. The wild is abundant with sources of protein if you know where and what to look for. Remember that you are specifically not focusing on hunting for animals. While it's true that animals are protein-rich food sources in the wild, there are various reasons you might opt for foraging instead. Ethical considerations, sustainability, the skill and physical strength required for hunting, as well as the potential dangers involved are just a few factors to bear in mind.

Foraging and hunting are fundamentally different practices. Hunting, as the term suggests, involves actively seeking and killing animals for food, often requiring specialized skills, tools, and significant energy expenditure. It's also worth noting that hunting often has a higher environmental impact compared to foraging.

The focus of this chapter is on foraging, not hunting, for protein-rich foods - a vital part of your diet that helps keep your body strong and healthy.

Why Do Humans Need Protein?

Before delving into the reasons behind foraging for protein, let's take a moment to understand what protein is and why it's important. In the simplest terms, proteins are the building blocks of life. They are vital for our growth and maintenance, involved in virtually every function of the cells. From repairing tissues to making enzymes and hormones, proteins are crucial for health. They are also a source of energy, providing about four calories per gram.

When you are low in protein, your body can experience a variety of negative impacts. For example, a protein deficiency can lead to muscle wasting, as the body starts to break down its muscle tissue to get the protein it needs. It can also weaken our immune system, making us more susceptible to illnesses. In children, a lack of protein can hinder growth and development. Hence, having a reliable source of protein in our diets is fundamental.

Insects as a Source of Protein

When you think of protein, your mind often gravitates towards meats like beef, chicken, or pork and dairy products. These animal-based sources of protein are indeed rich and contain all the essential amino acids that our bodies require, which are often referred to as complete proteins. This completeness and the high protein content found in meat are hard to match. However, there are other protein sources that are also protein-rich and abundant in the wild.

The most common examples are nuts and seeds, such as acorns, that have been a staple food source for indigenous communities across North America for centuries, and a single serving can contain roughly 6 grams of protein. Another source could be wild plants. While plant-based proteins, often found in various wild seeds and legumes, play an important role in our diet, they generally don't match the protein density found in animal-based sources. These plant proteins are often incomplete, meaning they lack some essential amino acids that the body needs.

As you push the boundaries of your diet and explore sustainable food sources, there is one group of creatures we've largely overlooked - insects. Often met with squirms and raised eyebrows, insects are an excellent, underappreciated source of protein. In fact, they are a regular part of the diet in many parts of the world. In countries like Thailand, Cambodia, and Vietnam, insects are common in dishes and usually sold in markets or served as street food. Silkworms, crickets, and various kinds of beetles are often fried and served as tasty, protein-rich snacks. In fact, in Thailand, a certain type of cricket known as "jing leed" is popular and is typically seasoned with soy sauce, sugar, and pepper before being deep-fried.

Why Choose Insects?

It might feel strange to consider insects as food, given the Western world's aversion to them. However, entomophagy, or the practice of eating insects, is common, and The Food and Agriculture Organization of the United Nations suggests insects can be a key player in global food security as they are:

Nutrient-rich

Insects are a fantastic source of protein, often outmatching traditional sources like beef and chicken. For instance, a cricket can have up to twice the protein of beef when compared pound for pound. They also provide essential amino acids, the building blocks of proteins, necessary for bodies to function optimally. Beyond protein, insects are rich in nutrients such as iron, zinc, and essential fatty acids. They offer a cocktail of nutrition in a small, crunchy package.

Sustainable

Raising insects requires fewer resources and produces fewer greenhouse gases than traditional livestock. They require less land, water, and food and can thrive on organic waste, making them an incredibly sustainable food source.

Plentiful

It's said that insects are the most numerous group of organisms on Earth. It's estimated that at any given time, there are some ten quintillion (that's 10 with 18 zeros!) individual insects alive. They inhabit nearly every ecosystem, from the deepest soils to the highest peaks, from the hottest deserts to the coldest tundras, and everything in between.

In practical terms, this means that wherever you are, there's a good chance that there are edible insects nearby. In a forest, they could be under logs or among the leaf litter. In a meadow, they might be hiding in the grass or on plants. Even in cities, edible insects can often be found in parks or other green spaces.

Types of Edible Insects

Now that you know why you should consider insects, it's time to look at the ones you can add to your plate.

Crickets

Crickets are a great 'starter insect' for beginners due to their mild taste. They're packed with protein and have a nice, nutty flavor when cooked. They typically have a body length of 0.12 to 2 inches and come in colors ranging from light brown to black. Key identifiers include their long, thin antennae, cylindrical bodies, and large hind legs adapted for jumping. Additionally, male crickets are known for their distinctive chirping sound, created by rubbing their wings together.

They're usually found in grassy fields and meadows but can also be found in gardens and other urban green spaces. You can capture them with a sweep net.

Mealworms

Mealworms, the larvae of darkling beetles, are another protein-rich option. They are typically golden brown in color and have a segmented, worm-like appearance. Mealworms can be anywhere from 0.5 to 1.2 inches long and have a hard outer shell.

You can find them in dark, damp areas like under logs or in compost. Simply sift through the material with gloves to collect them.

Grasshoppers

Grasshoppers are larger and more robust compared to crickets, with a size ranging from 1 to 7 inches. They're commonly found in shades of green and brown, which helps them blend into grassy environments. Grasshoppers have short antennae compared to crickets, and their powerful hind legs enable them to leap great distances.

Like crickets, grasshoppers are protein-dense and can be found in similar environments. They're often the most active and easiest to catch in the early morning when the cooler temperatures slow them down.

Ants

There are over 12,000 known species of ants worldwide, and many of them are safe to eat. Ants can vary widely in size, but they generally have a distinctive tri-segmented body structure consisting of the head, thorax, and abdomen. Most ants are small, typically less than 1 inch in length, and come in colors ranging from black to brown, red, or even yellow.

Species like the honeypot ant are rich in protein and have a unique, sweet taste. Ants can be found in virtually all environments but collecting them requires caution as some ants can bite or sting. Always exercise caution when foraging for ants.

Identifying Edible Insects

Not all insects are safe to eat, and consuming the wrong ones can lead to unpleasant or even dangerous consequences. Here are some tips on distinguishing between edible insects and those best left alone.

Know the Safe Species

The first step in identifying edible insects is learning about the species that are safe to eat. Many field guides and online resources can help you familiarize yourself with edible insects in your area. Crickets, grasshoppers, ants, and mealworms, which I've mentioned previously, are generally safe to eat but always make sure you've correctly identified any insect before consuming. Here are the next three most common inedible insects you may encounter.

Centipedes and Millipedes

These many-legged creatures are not safe to eat. Centipedes, which are often venomous, have one pair of legs per body segment. Millipedes, which can release irritating chemicals, have two pairs of legs per body segment.

Arachnids

This group includes spiders, scorpions, mites, and ticks. Although some cultures do consume certain arachnids, they are generally best avoided unless you are an expert. Many arachnids are venomous or parasitic.

Beetles

While some beetles, like the aforementioned darkling beetles, are safe to eat, many are not. Many beetles store toxins in their bodies and can be harmful if consumed.

Avoid Bright Colors

In nature, bright colors often serve as a warning. This is particularly true for many insects, where an array of striking colors serves a survival purpose rather than aesthetic appeal. This strategy, often referred to as "aposematism," is commonly employed by poisonous or harmful insects. Their bright coloration is a clear signal to potential predators that they are not a safe meal option, and it's an effective way to deter attacks.

This can be seen across various species that use their coloration as a deterrent. such as brightly colored beetles, butterflies, and wasps. Even within the same species, insects that are more toxic tend to exhibit brighter colors than their less toxic counterparts.

However, there are exceptions, and not all harmful insects are brightly colored. As a precautionary measure though, avoiding brightly colored insects can significantly decrease the risk of encountering harmful or poisonous varieties.

Steer Clear of Strong Smells

Many insects release strong odors as a defense mechanism. These stinky secretions are frequently a telltale sign that the insect may not be safe for consumption. The smell is essentially a biochemical warning to predators, including humans, communicating a clear message: "I am not good to eat."

Therefore, if you find an insect and it releases an intense, disagreeable odor upon handling, it is recommended to let it be. This doesn't just apply to those insects with smells that are immediately repulsive. Even if the smell isn't particularly unpleasant to you, it's still an important sign that the insect may have defenses that make it unsuitable for eating.

Beware of Stingers and Biters

Insects with stingers or strong mandibles (biting jaws) can be harmful. While some ants are edible, many have painful bites or stings. Bees and wasps, which are close relatives of ants, have stingers and are generally not safe to eat.

In Case of Uncertainty, Avoid Consumption

Consuming a misidentified insect can be dangerous. When in doubt, it's always best to prioritize safety, leave the insect alone and refrain from eating it.

Tips for Foraging insects

Here are a few tips to help you as you start your insect-foraging adventure:

- Early morning or late evening are usually the best times to catch insects, as many are less active then.
- Be patient and gentle. Rapid movements can startle insects and make them harder to catch.
- Use appropriate tools. A sweep net can be very useful when dealing with grass-dwelling insects.
- Wear protective clothing, especially gloves, to protect yourself from bites or stings.

Enjoying Insects

You've donned your forager's hat and identified and collected some edible insects. What's next? Let's walk through the process of cleaning, preparing, and cooking with your insect harvest.

Cleaning Your Insect Harvest

Proper cleaning is an essential first step after you've collected your insects. This step ensures you get rid of any dirt or bacteria they may carry. Here's how to go about it:

1. **Starve the Insects:** To purge their systems of any potential toxins they've ingested, keep your insects in a ventilated container with no food for 24 hours before you intend to cook them.
2. **Rinse Well:** After the fasting period, rinse the insects thoroughly under cold running water. This helps to remove any debris or dirt from their bodies.
3. **Boil:** Briefly boiling the insects can further help with cleaning. It also makes the insects safer to eat by killing potential parasites. After boiling, be sure to rinse the insects one more time.

Cooking Insects

Now that your insects are clean, you're ready to cook them! Cooking methods for insects can be as simple or as creative as you'd like. After your insects are thoroughly cleaned, consider these cooking options:

- **Roasting:** This is perhaps the simplest way to cook insects. Spread them out on a baking sheet, drizzle with a little oil, sprinkle with your favorite spices, and roast in the oven until crispy.

- **Frying:** For a quick and tasty option, try frying your insects in a bit of oil over medium-high heat. They'll become crunchy and golden in just a few minutes. Add a sprinkle of salt or other seasonings, and they're ready to eat.
- **Grinding:** You can dry your insects and then grind them into a fine powder to create insect flour. This can be a versatile ingredient in your kitchen, used in everything from baking to protein shakes.
- **Insect Flour:** One common way to use insects like crickets or mealworms is to grind them into flour. This can be used in place of traditional flour in recipes like bread, pancakes, or cookies. This is a great way to incorporate the nutritional benefits of insects into your diet without the crunch.

Embracing insects as a food source requires you to rethink your definitions of what food can be. It pushes you to step outside your comfort zones and embrace something unfamiliar. It might seem strange at first, but remember that every food you enjoy today was once a new discovery.

Who knows? With an open mind and adventurous spirit, you might find that these little critters can be a delightful, nutritious addition to your diet. As with any foraging, it's essential to prioritize safety and sustainability. Always properly identify any insect before consuming, cook thoroughly, and forage in a way that respects and protects shared natural spaces.

The world of insect foraging is rich and diverse, offering a sustainable and protein-rich alternative to traditional sources. So, why not give it a try?

Foraging Eggs

When I mention foraging eggs, I am not speaking about your typical chicken eggs from a farm. Rather, I'm talking about the diverse range of eggs found in the wild, from birds to reptiles, each providing a unique taste and culinary experience.

However, foraging for eggs isn't as straightforward as it sounds. It's a delicate practice that requires patience, knowledge, and respect for wildlife. You also have to respect the environment and avoid disturbing nesting sites. Remember, your foraging activities should never endanger the survival of any species. Also, make sure you can positively identify the species before you collect its eggs to ensure it's not endangered or protected.

With that out of the way, here is a comprehensive guide to help you forage protein-rich eggs.

The Safety of Wild Eggs

Safety is of utmost importance when foraging for and consuming wild eggs. Although they can be a delightful and unique culinary experience, they also come with certain risks if not properly identified and handled.

Generally, most bird eggs and some reptile eggs are safe to consume as long as they are collected responsibly, handled properly, and cooked thoroughly. However, just like with any wild food, there can be potential dangers.

One risk factor is exposure to pathogens. Wild animals can carry various diseases that can be passed on through their eggs. The most common one is salmonella, a bacterium that can cause severe food poisoning. Thorough cooking can kill these bacteria, which is why it's always recommended to cook wild eggs fully.

Another potential risk is chemical contamination, especially if the eggs are sourced from polluted environments. Eggs of wild birds or reptiles living in areas with high pollution, such as in the city, may be contaminated with harmful substances.

How to Determine if a Wild Egg is Safe to Eat

Determining the safety of a wild egg involves a couple of steps.

1. **Species identification:** You must know the species the egg came from. This will help you determine whether the egg is legally and ethically appropriate to forage. Also, certain species' eggs might not be suitable for consumption due to potential toxicity or strong flavors.
2. **Egg condition:** Check the condition of the egg. It should have an intact shell without cracks or leaks. Damaged eggs could be infected with bacteria or other pathogens.
3. **The Float Test:** This simple test can help determine the freshness of an egg. Place the egg in a bowl of water. Fresh eggs will sink, while older eggs will float due to a buildup of gas inside them. However, this test doesn't guarantee the egg is safe to eat. It should always be coupled with other checks.
4. **Smell and Visual Inspection:** Once cracked open, inspect the egg visually and by smell. Fresh eggs should have a neutral smell. If it smells foul, it's likely spoiled. The yolk should be a rich color and not broken, and the egg white should have a thick and thin part.
5. **Cooking:** Once you've responsibly collected your eggs, it's time to enjoy them. Wild eggs offer unique flavors that vary depending on the species and diet of the creature that produced them. They can be prepared in the same ways as common chicken eggs: boiled, scrambled, poached, or even used in baking. Remember always to cook wild eggs thoroughly to eliminate any potential bacteria. Avoid recipes where eggs are partially cooked or raw.

Tools for Egg Foraging

Egg foraging doesn't require an arsenal of tools. Like I've mentioned earlier, a good pair of boots, long-sleeved clothing, a basket or pouch to collect your findings, and a guidebook of local fauna are the basics. But another essential accessory is a pair of binoculars, useful for spotting nests from a distance and reducing disturbance to wildlife.

Identifying Nests

Identifying and locating nests in the wild can be quite a challenge, especially for those new to foraging. Birds, reptiles, and other egg-laying creatures are exceptionally skilled at camouflaging their nests to protect them from predators. Here's a deeper look into how you can enhance your nest-spotting skills, complete with examples.

Know Your Local Species

The first step is to familiarize yourself with the fauna of your local area. Are there a lot of waterfowl, pigeons, or quails? Maybe turtles are abundant in nearby ponds? Understanding what species live in your region will give you an idea of what kind of nests to look for.

For instance, pigeons typically build rudimentary nests in trees or on buildings using twigs and other debris. On the other hand, quails are ground-nesters, laying their eggs in simple scrapes lined with vegetation. Turtles, being reptiles, bury their eggs in sandy or soft soil, usually close to a water body.

You can learn about the local species by using online databases or nature guides. Observing the species in their natural habitat will also provide valuable insights into their behavior, including nesting habits.

Understand Nesting Habits

Different species have different nesting habits. Some birds, like eagles and hawks, prefer high, inaccessible places like treetops or cliff faces. Others, like sparrows and finches, might choose safer, more concealed areas within shrubs or dense foliage.

Waterfowl such as ducks and geese often build nests near water bodies hidden in tall grass or reeds. Reptiles like turtles and lizards lay their eggs in burrows or soft soil and cover them with sand or dirt.

Observing and Recognize Nests

Now that you're familiar with the local species and their nesting habits, it's time to hit the field. Remember, patience is key. Nest spotting requires time and careful observation.

Look for signs such as bird droppings or feathers, which can indicate a nest above. Watch the behavior of birds; they often reveal their nests' location through their coming and going. For reptiles, look for disturbed soil or sand, which could indicate a buried nest.

Keep in mind that some nests will be easy to spot, like a pigeon's nest in a tree, while others will be harder like a quail's nest camouflaged against the ground. Always use binoculars for observation to keep disturbance to a minimum.

Different Types of Wild Eggs

In the wild, numerous species lay eggs, but for the purpose of foraging, They can broadly categorize these into two main types: bird eggs and reptile eggs. Each category holds a myriad of species, each with unique habits, habitats, and, of course, eggs.

Bird Eggs

The bird eggs most commonly foraged are those of wildfowl, pigeons, or quails. In rural settings, turkey, duck, and goose eggs might also be found. Always follow ethical guidelines and only forage from species that aren't threatened or endangered.

Remember, different bird species lay eggs at different times of the year. For example, quail eggs are usually found in spring, while pigeon eggs can be found throughout the year.

Reptile Eggs

If you live in an area with a large reptile population, foraging reptile eggs can be an exciting adventure. Reptile eggs, such as those of turtles or certain lizards, are often buried underground or hidden in vegetation.

Turtle eggs, for example, are typically laid in sandy nests near bodies of water. If you happen to come across a nest, ensure the species isn't endangered and be extra careful not to disturb the surrounding area.

Chapter 5
Fungi

Fungi. It's a word that might evoke images of the mushrooms you add to your salad or pasta, but there's much more to these peculiar organisms than meets the eye. They might not have the vibrant allure of blooming flowers or the grandeur of towering trees, yet fungi are a vital part of the world. They are the unsung heroes of ecosystems, working tirelessly beneath the surface and performing critical tasks that contribute to life.

Fungi play a starring role in nature's cycle of life and death. They are the Earth's recyclers, breaking down organic material like leaves and dead trees, turning them into rich soil that provides the essential nutrients for plants to grow. Without fungi, forests and gardens would be littered with the accumulated waste of seasons past. They are the quiet, dependable workers that keep the circle of life turning.

In this chapter, I'll introduce you to the variety of types that exist. I aim to help you recognize the differences between edible and poisonous fungi. I'll share with you techniques on identifying edible fungi, such as noting their physical characteristics and growing conditions. Finally, you'll learn the benefits and risks associated with foraging fungi. From their health benefits to potential dangers, it's essential to be well-informed.

A Closer Look on Fungi

When you hear the term 'fungi,' what first comes to mind? For many, it's the classic umbrella-shaped structure you might recognize as a mushroom. But there's a whole hidden universe to fungi that you often overlook.

Firstly, fungi aren't plants. They belong to their own kingdom altogether, separate from plants and animals. Imagine a kingdom teeming with organisms that have the power to decompose organic material, produce delicious food, and even help brew beer. That's the realm of fungi.

At the heart of a fungus lies a network of thin threads known as hyphae. These hyphae form the body of the fungus called the mycelium and play a critical role in absorbing nutrients from the environment. Unlike plants, fungi don't photosynthesize. Instead, they get their nutrition from the organic material they break down in their surroundings.

The mushroom or mold you see above ground? That's just the tip of the iceberg. Most of a fungus's life takes place out of sight, beneath the surface, with the mycelium hard at work. When conditions are right, some fungi produce the structures we're familiar with (like mushrooms) as a way to distribute their spores and reproduce.

Types of Fungi

Fungi are a diverse bunch, with hundreds of thousands of species known to science and many more yet to be discovered. They come in all shapes, sizes, and colors, each with their unique traits. Let's take a quick tour through the kingdom of fungi, focusing on three commonly known types: mushrooms, sac fungi, and molds.

Mushrooms

Mushrooms are likely the first image that pops up in your mind when you hear "fungi." Belonging to the class Agaricomycetes, mushrooms are particularly recognizable due to their familiar structure comprising a cap, gills, and a stem.

The cap varies in shape and color, ranging from flat to conical, and can be any color of the rainbow. Gills are found under the cap, radiating outwards from the stem. These gills house the spores, which are eventually released to form new mushrooms.

Common Examples

- **Portobello, Crimini, and White Button (Agaricus bisporus):** These are essentially the same species at different maturity stages. They are often found in grasslands and have a cap that's creamy white to brown, with gills that darken as they mature. They're safe to eat and popular in culinary use.
- **Fly Agaric (Amanita muscaria):** With its bright red cap dotted with white spots, this mushroom is iconic. However, it's toxic and should not be consumed. It's commonly found in woodland and heath areas.
- **Chanterelle (Cantharellus cibarius):** These have a distinctive funnel shape and egg-yolk yellow color, often found in woodland areas. Chanterelles are prized for their delicious taste.
- **Puffball (Lycoperdon perlatum):** Puffballs are usually round or pear-shaped and lack the typical cap and stem structure of most mushrooms. Instead, they are characterized by their smooth, white exterior that turns brownish as they mature. When ripe, they release a cloud of spores, giving them their "puffball" name.

Sac Fungi

Sac fungi, or Ascomycetes, are named for the "ascus," a sac-like structure that contains spores. These fungi can have various forms, ranging from single-celled yeasts to complex cup and morel mushrooms. Their diverse forms are unified by the presence of the ascus.

In particular, morels (Morchella species) stand as a remarkable representative of sac fungi. The whimsical shape, akin to a honeycomb or sponge, sets them apart from other fungi. Colors generally range from golden yellow to dark brown. The cap's pits and ridges are not just aesthetically unique but serve a purpose, creating a large surface area for spore release. This trait, combined with their rich, nutty flavor, makes morels a favorite among foragers.

Common Examples

- **Scarlet Elf Cup (Sarcoscypha austriaca).** Found on decaying sticks and branches, the Scarlet Elf Cup lives up to its name with vibrant, red, cup-shaped fruit bodies. The outer surface is often covered with a white layer of hair, adding to its distinctive look.
- **Black Truffle (Tuber melanosporum).** The Black Truffle is a gourmet delight found underground near the roots of certain trees. Its outer skin is black and warty, while the inside is marbled with white veins.

Molds

Though molds aren't typically on a forager's list, understanding them can add another layer to your ecological knowledge. Molds span across various fungal classes, primarily acting as nature's decomposers. Their bodies, largely composed of thread-like hyphae, may appear as a fuzzy or powdery film of organic matter. Coloration can be stark white, deep green, or even jet black.

Molds break down dead matter, transforming a fallen log or overripe fruit into a buffet of nutrients for other organisms. Recognizing the presence of mold can also be crucial when foraging. Moldy fruit or a mushroom touched by mold is a clear indicator of over-ripening or decay, signaling that it's not suitable for consumption.

Uses of Fungi

The world of fungi is far-reaching and full of surprises. Whether you're foraging in the wild for a culinary treat, brewing your own beer, or simply appreciating the role of fungi in our ecosystem, it's clear that these incredible organisms offer countless benefits and uses. Here is a more specific look at how fungi are used in different aspects of life.

Food and Cooking

When it comes to food, fungi take center stage in a variety of dishes around the globe. The rich and diverse flavors, textures, and nutritional benefits of fungi make them a staple in many kitchens.

Familiar fungi like the Chanterelle, Morel, and Porcini mushrooms are used in countless dishes for their unique flavors. They're packed with nutrients, low in calories, and high in fiber and protein. While Black and white truffles, the hidden gems of the fungal world, are highly sought after for their unique, intoxicating aroma. They're often used in gourmet dishes, imparting a luxurious touch. Lastly, Saccharomyces cerevisiae, or baker's yeast, is a crucial ingredient in baking. It's responsible for the leavening of bread, creating its fluffy, light texture.

Natural Remedies

Fungi also play a significant role in natural medicine, demonstrating healing properties that have been recognized and used for centuries. Here are some examples:

- **Reishi:** This mushroom, also known as Ganoderma lucidum, has been used in traditional Asian medicine for its immune-boosting and anti-cancer properties.
- **Cordyceps:** Cordyceps fungi are renowned for their potential to increase energy levels, endurance, and overall athletic performance.
- **Chaga:** The Chaga mushroom, found on birch trees, is packed with antioxidants and is often consumed as a tea for its potential health benefits.

Industrial Uses

Finally, let's not forget the part fungi play in various industries such as.

- **Production of antibiotics:** The Penicillium mold is famous for the production of penicillin, the world's first antibiotic. It marked a revolution in modern medicine, saving countless lives.
- **Cheese production:** Fungi like Penicillium roqueforti and Penicillium camemberti are used to produce cheeses like Roquefort and Camembert, contributing to their characteristic flavors and textures.
- **Brewing:** Yeasts, particularly Saccharomyces cerevisiae, play a crucial role in brewing beer and producing wine, where they ferment sugars to produce alcohol.

Foraging Fungi Safely

Misidentification of fungi can lead to serious consequences. In this section, I'll discuss how to distinguish between edible and poisonous mushrooms and outline some essential dos and don'ts when foraging for these.

Possible Effects of Consuming Poisonous Mushrooms

While many mushrooms are safe to eat, there are a few notorious ones that can cause severe illness or even be fatal if consumed. Here's a closer look at what could happen if you accidentally ingest a poisonous mushroom.

Gastrointestinal Upset

One of the most common effects of consuming poisonous mushrooms is gastrointestinal distress. Symptoms usually occur within a few hours of ingestion and may include nausea, vomiting, abdominal cramps, and diarrhea. While these symptoms can be extremely uncomfortable, they often resolve on their own within a day or two. However, severe cases may require medical treatment to prevent dehydration.

Liver and Kidney Damage

Some of the most dangerous mushrooms, such as the Death Cap (Amanita phalloides), contain toxins that can cause severe damage to the liver and kidneys. Symptoms may not appear until several hours or even a day after ingestion, beginning as gastrointestinal upset but then progressing to more serious complications. If not treated promptly, this can lead to liver or kidney failure and can be fatal.

Neurological Effects

Certain poisonous mushrooms can affect the nervous system. The Fly Agaric (Amanita muscaria), for example, contains psychoactive compounds that can cause hallucinations, confusion, and agitation. Other symptoms might include muscle weakness, difficulty coordinating movements, and seizures.

Delayed Onset of Symptoms

Some mushroom toxins may not cause symptoms for several hours to days after ingestion, which can make it difficult for the person affected (or even medical professionals) to link the symptoms to mushroom poisoning. This delay makes these types of poisonings particularly dangerous.

If you suspect that you or someone else has consumed a poisonous mushroom, seek medical attention immediately. If possible, bring a sample of the mushroom(s) that were consumed to aid in identification and treatment.

Common Poisonous Fungi

Here, you'll take a look at some of these deadly species that you may come across in the wild. The descriptions provided here are only a general guide, and numerous other poisonous fungi exist in the wild. I know you might be tired of hearing this, but If in doubt, it's best to leave it alone. No foraged meal is worth risking your health or life for.

Amanita phalloides

One of the most lethal mushrooms globally, the Death Cap, accounts for a high percentage of fatal mushroom poisonings. It's often mistaken for edible species due to its innocent appearance.

It has a smooth, glossy, and greenish-yellow cap, which can vary in color from olive to brown. Its gills are white, as is its stem, which also has a skirt-like ring and a bulbous base. The Death Cap has a wide distribution and can be found in various woodland habitats.

Amanita muscaria

The Fly Agaric, with its distinctive bright red cap with white spots, is one of the most iconic mushrooms. Despite its fairy-tale appearance, it's psychoactive and can cause various symptoms if consumed, ranging from nausea and dizziness to hallucinations. While not as deadly as the Death Cap, it's still best avoided.

Galerina marginata

This small and inconspicuous mushroom is another potentially deadly species. Often found on decaying wood, it has a brown cap with gills and a stem of similar color. Its size and color make it easy to overlook or mistake for a harmless variety.

Gyromitra esculenta

False Morels, as their name implies, can look strikingly similar to the highly sought-after true Morels, but consuming them can be fatal. They have a brain-like or wrinkled cap that is brown to dark brown. They're found in sandy soils, particularly in coniferous forests.

Clitocybe dealbata

This mushroom is small and white, often with a slightly convex or flat cap. The Deadly Angel can be found growing in grassy areas, such as lawns or pastures. Consuming this mushroom can lead to muscarine poisoning, characterized by symptoms such as sweating, salivation, and blurred vision.

Distinguishing Edible Mushrooms

Though I have discussed three common types of fungi, I'll focus on mushroom identification as it's the most commonly foraged fungi and has the most edible and poisonous species. Identifying these mushrooms is a skill honed over time and with experience. While there are no foolproof rules, there are some general tips that can guide you:

Familiarize Yourself with the Fungi

I cannot stress enough the importance of learning about the common edible and poisonous species in your local area. Not only do you learn about the incredible diversity of fungi around you, but you also improve your chances of identifying edible species and avoiding poisonous ones. As I said before, you can invest in a good field guide that is specific to your region. These guides often have detailed descriptions, clear photographs, and notes about the habitat and growth conditions of each species. They may also include warnings about similar-looking poisonous species. There are also numerous websites and apps that can assist with mushroom identification. However, be wary of using them as they can be misleading or inaccurate. Remember to use them with caution, though, as they should complement, not replace, field guides and expert advice.

Aside from this, you can try joining a local mycological society or a foraging group. Experienced members can help you identify specimens during foraging expeditions and share their insights and knowledge. They often organize guided foraging walks, workshops, and presentations - all excellent opportunities for learning.

Checking the Entire Mushroom

Once you have gathered the mushrooms, you must examine all parts of the mushroom to ensure correct identification. Every part can provide critical information that brings you closer to a safe and accurate identification. Here's a quick guide on what to look out for:

- **Cap:** The shape, color, texture, and any markings or changes in color are important. Is it flat, convex, or concave? Is it smooth, scaly, or slimy? Does it have warts or other markings?
- **Gills/Pores:** Are there gills under the cap, or are there pores, or perhaps spikes? What color are they? Do they change color when bruised? The arrangement and attachment of the gills to the stem can also be a key characteristic.
- **Stem**: The color, shape, thickness, length, and texture of the stem can all aid in identification. Does it have a ring (also known as an annulus)? Is it solid or hollow? Is the base bulbous or tapered?
- **Base:** The base can sometimes be hidden underground, so careful excavation might be necessary. Some mushrooms, like certain Amanitas, have a distinctive volva or "egg" at the base of the stem, which is a critical identification feature.

Check the Spore Prints

The spore print is often overlooked, yet it's one of the most reliable methods for identifying a mushroom. Fungi reproduce by releasing spores, tiny particles that can be thought of as seeds. Different species of mushrooms produce different colored spores, which can be a vital identifying characteristic.

To make a spore print, you need a mature mushroom, a piece of paper (white and black can be helpful to accommodate different spore colors), and a glass or a bowl to cover the mushroom. Remove the stem from the mushroom and place the cap, gill-side-down, on the paper. Cover it with a glass or bowl to prevent air currents from disturbing the spores. After a few hours or overnight, remove the glass and the cap. You should have a spore print. If you want a more in-depth instructions on this, proceed to the end of the chapter for an activity involving making your own spore print.

The color of the spore print can help distinguish between similar-looking species. For instance, the edible Field Mushroom (Agaricus campestris) and the toxic Yellow-staining Mushroom (Agaricus xanthodermus) can look similar. Still, their spore prints are different colors - brown for the Field Mushroom and yellow for the Yellow-staining Mushroom.

Note the Growing and Ground Conditions

Knowing where to look and what to look for when it comes to fungi growth conditions can be instrumental in making a correct identification between edible and poisonous mushrooms. To help you identify whether a mushroom is poisonous, you can ask these questions:

Where is the mushroom growing?

The substrate that a mushroom is growing on is often a good clue. Some mushrooms prefer to grow on dead or decaying wood, such as logs, stumps, or fallen branches. These are known as saprophytic fungi and include many edible species, such as Shiitake (Lentinula edodes) and Oyster mushrooms (Pleurotus ostreatus).

Others prefer to grow in the soil, feeding off decaying matter below the surface. Chanterelles (Cantharellus cibarius), for example, typically grow on the ground, often in mossy, damp conditions.

Then there are parasitic fungi, like the infamous Death Cap (Amanita phalloides), which grows on the roots of certain trees and can be deadly if consumed.

Understanding the terrain and soil conditions can also help you, as some mushrooms prefer sandy soils, while others favor clay or loamy soils. The soil's acidity or alkalinity can also affect where mushrooms choose to grow.

In addition to soil type, consider the surrounding conditions. Are you in a wet, marshy area or a dry, arid one? Fungi like the Slippery Jack (Suillus luteus) love damp, boggy areas, whereas the Desert Truffle (Terfezia boudieri) thrives in arid conditions.

Near which kind of tree?

Certain types of trees share distinctive relationships with fungi, particularly those classified as mycorrhizal fungi. These fungi enter into symbiotic partnerships with trees, playing a vital role in helping the trees access nutrients and water. In exchange for their services, these fungi receive sugars produced by the tree through photosynthesis.

For example, Porcini mushrooms (Boletus edulis) often grow near pine, oak, and birch trees. Morels (Morchella spp.) have a strong association with ash, elm, and apple trees, especially those that are dying or recently dead.

Don't Rely on Old Wives' Tales

In the world of foraging, various myths and misconceptions circulate, many of which can prove dangerously misleading. Among these, you'll find numerous "old wives' tales" offering supposedly easy ways to distinguish between edible and poisonous mushrooms. A couple of examples include the notion that "poisonous mushrooms tarnish silver" or "if it peels, it's safe."

Let's take a closer look at these and understand why relying on such folklore could potentially be hazardous.

Myth 1: Poisonous Mushrooms Tarnish Silver

This myth proposes that if you cook a poisonous mushroom with silverware or place a silver coin in the cooking pot, the silver will tarnish or change color. However, this is untrue and dangerously misleading. The reaction between silver and certain compounds found in mushrooms is not a reliable indicator of toxicity. Many harmless mushrooms can cause silver to tarnish, while many toxic mushrooms will not.

Myth 2: If it Peels, It's Safe

This myth is based on the idea that if the cap of a mushroom can be easily peeled, it must be safe to eat. Again, this is a dangerous misconception. While it's true that some edible mushroom species have caps that can be peeled, this is also the case for several poisonous species. For instance, the deadly poisonous Death Cap (Amanita phalloides) has a peelable cap.

When in Doubt, Leave it Out

As I've previously discussed, one of the key tenets of foraging, particularly for beginners, is this: Refrain from consuming any mushroom if its identification isn't absolutely certain. The potential dangers far outweigh the benefits.

It is a common occurrence for even the most seasoned foragers to stumble upon mushroom species they aren't able to identify with certainty. In these circumstances, they abide by this principle.

Keep in mind that the consumption of certain toxic mushrooms can result in severe sickness or even fatality. A few may not be lethal, but they are capable of producing unpleasant symptoms such as nausea, upset stomach, and abdominal discomfort.

Furthermore, remember that even after confirming a mushroom is safe to consume, individual reactions can vary widely across different species. It's advisable to initially ingest a minimal quantity and monitor any adverse reactions before consuming a larger portion.

How to Cook and Prepare Foraged Fungi

Having a successful foraging trip is a thrilling experience. You've identified and collected a variety of fungi, and now it's time to enjoy the fruits (or, more accurately, the fungi) of your labor. Here are some simple and practical ways to cook and prepare your foraged fungi in the wild.

Inspect and Clean Your Foraged Fungi

The first step after foraging is inspecting and cleaning your fungi. Brush off any dirt or debris gently with a soft brush. Avoid washing them as they can easily absorb water and become soggy. Cut the mushrooms in half lengthwise to inspect the insides for any signs of decay or infestation.

Sautéed Wild Mushrooms

Sautéing is one of the simplest and most popular ways to prepare wild mushrooms. It's straightforward and allows the unique flavors of the mushrooms to shine through.

1. **Heat the Cooking Surface.** If you're in the wild, this could be a portable camping stove or an open fire. A cast-iron pan is perfect for this task. Heat the pan and add a dollop of butter or a splash of cooking oil.
2. **Add the Mushrooms.** Once the butter has melted or the oil is shimmering, add your sliced mushrooms.
3. **Cook Until Golden.** Cook the mushrooms, stirring occasionally, until they're tender and golden brown. This usually takes around 10-15 minutes.
4. **Add flavoring.** Season with salt and any herbs you may have brought along. Wild thyme or garlic works great with most wild mushrooms.

Grilled Wild Mushrooms

Grilling is another excellent method for cooking wild mushrooms, especially larger ones like Portobello or puffballs.

1. **Prepare the Mushrooms.** Clean your mushrooms and leave them whole or slice them if they're large. Drizzle with olive oil and season with salt and pepper.

2. **Grill.** Place the mushrooms on the grill, cap side down first. Cook for about 5 minutes on each side until they're nicely charred and cooked through.
3. **Serve.** You can serve these grilled mushrooms as they are or add a squeeze of lemon for extra flavor.

Steamed Wild Mushrooms

Steaming is a gentle cooking method that can help preserve delicate flavors in your foraged mushrooms.

1. **Prepare Your Steaming Setup.** This could be a steamer basket in a pot of boiling water or even a makeshift steamer made of tin foil with holes poked in it placed over a pot of water.
2. **Steam the Mushrooms.** Add the mushrooms to your steamer and cover. Steam until the mushrooms are tender, about 10 minutes depending on their size.
3. **Season and Serve.** Season the steamed mushrooms with salt, pepper, and a drizzle of olive oil or a pat of butter.

Always remember that no matter how you prepare and cook your mushrooms, they must be fully cooked. Raw wild mushrooms are hard to digest and may contain harmful bacteria or compounds. Moreover, some wild mushrooms can only be eaten safely after they're properly cooked.

Exercise: Fungi Spore Print Making

Creating spore prints is an exciting and visual way to explore the world of fungi without needing to identify specific species. It captures the unique pattern of a mushroom's spores and can sometimes be used in identification. But in this exercise, you'll be focusing on the process and the beautiful prints that can result. It's an excellent activity for all ages!

Materials Required
- Mushrooms (freshly picked; remember to use gloves and avoid poisonous mushrooms)
- Paper (white and black can help display different spore colors)
- Glasses or jars (to cover the mushrooms)
- Tweezers

1. **Prepare the Mushroom.** Choose a mature mushroom and carefully cut off the stem to make it lay flat. It's important to note that immature mushrooms may not drop spores effectively, so look for fully-opened caps.
2. **Make the Spore Print.** Place the cap gill-side down on a piece of paper. To get the best results, you can split the cap between two contrasting colors, like white and black. Some spores are white and will show better on dark paper, while others may be dark-colored.
3. **Cover and Wait.** Cover the mushroom cap with a glass or jar. This helps to prevent air currents from disturbing the spore drop and maintains a humid environment that encourages the mushroom to release its spores.
4. **Observe and Preserve the Print.** Leave the mushroom undisturbed for at least several hours, ideally overnight. After enough time has passed, carefully lift the cover and use the tweezers to pick up the mushroom cap Underneath, you should find a beautiful spore print! Each species of mushroom has a unique spore print, differing in color and pattern. To preserve your spore print, you can lightly spray it with hairspray or a similar fixative. Just remember to do this in a well-ventilated area.

Spore printing can be a fun and educational activity that gives you a tangible connection to the often-unseen world of fungi spores. Plus, the prints can be quite beautiful, and each one is unique. Enjoy discovering this aspect of fungi in a safe, creative way.

Chapter 6
Water Resource Foraging

When discussing water, I bet you often focus on its role as a life-sustaining drink. But there's much more to bodies of water than quenching thirst. They're also home to a wide array of aquatic plants that are not only edible but also packed with nutrients. These plants, often overlooked, can provide vital sustenance in survival situations and even form part of a regular diet.

In this chapter, you'll learn about foraging these aquatic treasures. I'll guide you on identifying edible aquatic plants or creatures, which ones to avoid, and how to harvest them sustainably. I'll also share tips on how to cook and store them for long-term use.

While the spotlight is on aquatic plant foraging, it's impossible to discuss this without addressing the basics of locating water sources. Water bodies are, after all, the habitat for these edible plants and creatures. I will share with you tips on locating bodies of water and a guide on how to identify healthy and potentially harmful water sources. Afterwards, I'll provide different ways of gathering and purifying water.

Aquatic Plant Foraging

When it comes to foraging, the imagery that comes to mind is wild berries, mushrooms, nuts, and other land-based resources. But shift your gaze from the forest floor to the vast bodies of water— the rivers, lakes, ponds, and even seas. Aquatic plant foraging, through identifying and harvesting edible plants from water bodies, opens up a whole new world of resources that are often ignored but are just as valuable.

They can be a surprising source of nutrition and sustenance. They are abundant in vitamins, proteins, and particularly minerals like iodine and selenium, which are found less often in land plants. They can also provide you with a balanced diet.

Types of Aquatic Plants

Aquatic Plants come in a wide variety, each with its unique characteristics, growth patterns, and nutritional profiles. These plants can be broadly categorized into three types: emergent, submerged, and floating plants.

Emergent plants, such as cattails and wild rice, have their roots firmly planted underwater. However, most of the plant, including its stem, leaves, and flowers, resides above the water's surface.

Submerged plants, as the name suggests, are entirely underwater. Examples include seaweeds and eelgrass.

Floating plants, such as water lilies and duckweed, float freely on the water's surface with their roots dangling in the water. The leaves of these plants are often broad and waxy to repel water and prevent sinking. They provide shade, reducing water temperature and sunlight penetration, which can inhibit excessive algal growth.

The variety of aquatic plants is as diverse as the land-based flora you're more familiar with. And just like their terrestrial counterparts, not all aquatic plants are edible or safe to consume.

The Role of Aquatic Plants in Survival and Sustenance

Aquatic plants are more than just beautiful elements in bodies of water; they play a crucial role in survival and sustenance. In survival scenarios where traditional food sources might be limited or unavailable, these plants can serve as a vital source of nutrition.

For example, consider the cattail. This emergent aquatic plant is often regarded as the *"supermarket of the swamp."* Almost all parts of the cattail are edible at various stages of its growth. The young shoots can be eaten raw or cooked, the yellow pollen can be used as a flour substitute, and the roots can be processed to extract a nutritious starch.

Similarly, seaweeds, a submerged plant, have been part of the human diet for centuries in many coastal cultures. They're rich in iodine, calcium, and other essential nutrients. Seaweeds like nori, kelp, and dulse can be eaten raw, cooked, or dried.

Aquatic plants not only serve as food sources but also as medicinal resources. For instance, the willowherb, often found near water bodies, has been used traditionally for its anti-inflammatory and antimicrobial properties.

When learning to forage aquatic plants, you are not just equipping yourself with a survival skill. Instead, you are expanding your food choices, learning to appreciate often overlooked resources, and promoting more sustainable, eco-friendly eating habits. It's a journey of discovery, resilience, and a return to our roots, intimately linked with water, the source of life.

Edible Aquatic Plants Habitats

The world beneath the water's surface is filled with a diversity of plants, some of which are edible and delicious. But to begin your foraging journey, you must first understand where these plants thrive. Identifying the habitat of common edible aquatic plants can lead you to a treasure trove of untapped food sources.

Freshwater bodies like rivers, streams, ponds, and lakes are home to various edible aquatic plants. For instance, cattails and wild rice predominantly grow in shallow water or marshy areas, usually around the edges of freshwater bodies. You can spot their tall, robust stems jutting above the water surface, with their roots anchored in the waterlogged soil.

In saltwater environments, such as oceans and seas, there are numerous edible species too. Seaweeds, a broad term encompassing various types of marine algae, are perhaps the most common and recognized edible sea plants. They are usually found attached to rocks, other hard substrates, or even other plants in intertidal zones and below the water's surface.

And then, there are aquatic plants that can thrive in both freshwater and saltwater environments. Duckweed, a tiny free-floating plant, can be found in calm ponds, lakes, and even slow-moving streams.

Most Common Edible Aquatic Plants

Identifying edible aquatic plants requires a keen eye for their physical characteristics. Let's consider a few examples.

- **Cattails (Typha spp.).** Look for tall, upright plants growing in or near the water when foraging for cattails. They can reach heights of up to 10 feet. Their leaves are long and flat, somewhat sword-like, arranged in a tight circular pattern around the stem. During spring and early summer, you can notice two parts of the inflorescence (flower cluster) developing on the stalk. The lower, thicker part develops into the familiar brown cylindrical structure, often described as 'hot dog' or 'sausage-shaped', and the narrower part above it forms a conical spike. While the entire plant is edible at various stages, the young shoots (spring) and roots (fall and winter) are most commonly harvested.

- **Wild Rice (Zizania spp.).** Wild rice plants stand out with their tall, gracefully arching stems that can reach heights of 6 to 9 feet. The leaves, about 1 to 2 inches wide, are long, slender, and tapering, with a distinct midrib. The stems are hollow and spongy. During the fall, look for large, branching flower clusters, or panicles, that bear the grains. These clusters start as green, turning to purple or purplish-black, and eventually, a golden brown when the grains are ripe and ready to harvest.
- **Duckweed (Lemna spp.).** Duckweed is the smallest flowering plant. Each plant, or frond, is a flat, oval structure, green in color, often just 1 to 3 millimeters in length. They float on the water's surface, often forming a dense green carpet. Underneath each frond hangs a single, translucent root (or rootlet) that can be 1 to 2 centimeters long. Despite their tiny size, they are rich in protein and have been utilized as a food source in various cultures.
- **Seaweeds**: Seaweeds are incredibly diverse, so let's focus on two commonly foraged varieties.
  - **Nori (Pyropia/ Porphyra spp.):** Nori is a type of red algae, although its color can range from dark red to black when dried. The plant forms thin, flat, sheet-like structures that can be 30 centimeters (about 1 foot) long or even more. They are commonly found attached to rocks in intertidal zones.

- **Kelp (Laminaria spp.):** Kelp is a brown algae found in colder oceanic waters. It has a complex structure with a root-like holdfast, a flexible stem-like stipe, and leaf-like blades. The blades are large, flat, and can be several meters long. The surface of the blade is smooth, and the edges can be either smooth or wavy.

Harmful Aquatic Plants

Venturing into the world of foraging aquatic plants offers a fascinating array of possibilities. But it's not just about identifying what you can eat; it's equally crucial to be aware of what you can't. Learning to recognize potentially harmful or poisonous aquatic plants is an essential part of a forager's education. Here, I'll outline some of the most common toxic aquatic plants that are best avoided.

- **Water Hemlock (Cicuta spp.).** Easily mistaken for a benign plant, the water hemlock is regarded as one of North America's most poisonous plants. Growing in marshy areas and along water edges, this plant can grow up to 2 meters tall, sporting clusters of small white flowers and finely divided, fern-like leaves. Its stem is hollow, and it has a characteristic root system with a swollen base full of yellowish oily liquid, which contains the deadly cicutoxin. Consumption of even a small part of this plant can lead to severe poisoning, resulting in seizures and possibly death.
- **Blue-Green Algae (Cyanobacteria).** Though technically not a plant but a bacteria, blue-green algae pose a significant threat in bodies of water, especially during warm weather when blooms occur. They can give the water a green, blue-green, or even reddish-brown appearance and may form scum on the water's surface. Certain species produce toxins harmful to both humans and animals, causing a range of symptoms from skin irritation to

severe stomach problems and, in extreme cases, damage to the liver and nervous system.

- **Foxglove (Digitalis purpurea).** While not truly aquatic, this plant is often found in damp habitats near water. It can be recognized by its tall, spike-like clusters of purple, bell-shaped flowers, and its large, downy leaves. Although beautiful, every part of the plant is toxic, with ingestion leading to heart palpitations, nausea, and potentially fatal heart complications.
- **Water Arum (Calla palustris).** It has a deceptive appearance that can be confusing. Its resemblance to popular wild edibles makes it easy for the untrained eye to mistake it for food. For instance, its spade-shaped leaves may remind you of common sorrel, while the bright green color and clustered growth might bring to mind wild leeks. It is found in swamps and marshes, with arrow-shaped leaves and a distinctive greenish-yellow flower spike surrounded by a white sheath. Consumption of any part of this plant, however, can lead to intense burning and irritation of the mouth and throat.

Toxicity Warning Signs

Understanding the common signs of plant toxicity can literally be a lifesaver. Aside from this, recognizing these signs can also help in maintaining the health of aquatic ecosystems. Because of these indicators, proper identification through field guides, expert consultation, or scientific analysis is always the safest approach when dealing with unknown aquatic plants. Some warning signs include:

- **Bitter or Soapy Taste.** Aquatic plants exhibiting a bitter or soapy taste could potentially be harmful. However, this method has limitations as taste can be subjective, and some non-toxic aquatic plants may also have similar taste profiles to poisonous ones. Furthermore, tasting un-

known plants can lead to accidental ingestion of toxins, so it is not generally recommended.
- **Algae Blooms.** Sudden, massive growth of algae in the water body can be a sign of high nutrient levels, often a result of runoffs from agriculture or sewage waste. While algae are a natural part of water ecosystems, excessive growth can deplete oxygen levels in the water, leading to anoxic conditions that can cause harm to both plants and animals.
- **Aquatic Plants with Bulbous Structures.** Certain aquatic plants contain bulbous parts that could be reservoirs for concentrated toxins. Bulbs often store energy and nutrients for the plant, including defensive chemicals. If an aquatic plant's specific identity is uncertain, direct contact or consumption of the plant, especially the bulbous parts, should be avoided due to the potential risk of toxicity. An example is the Water Hyacinth (Eichhornia crassipes) It is also known to accumulate toxins in its bulbous parts, which the plant uses as a defensive mechanism. It can be harmful to humans if ingested or come into direct contact with.
- **Presence of Dead Fish or Aquatic Animals:** If you notice dead fish or other aquatic animals in the water, it's a strong indication that the water may be toxic. Fish are more sensitive to changes in water quality, and their death could signify a larger problem.
- **Unpleasant Odors:** Some toxic conditions can result in unpleasant smells, such as a strong, foul, or rotten odor. This could be due to the breakdown of organic matter or the release of gases from certain types of pollutants.
- **Aquatic Plants in Contaminated Water.** Aquatic plants, like their terrestrial counterparts, have the ability to uptake and accumulate contaminants from the surrounding environment. Those growing in stagnant, polluted, or contaminated water may absorb harmful bacteria, heavy metals,

or other toxic chemicals. As such, these plants can pose a hazard to aquatic life and other organisms that come into contact with or consume them. This bioaccumulation can also serve as an indicator of water quality and help identify areas of pollution.

Foraging Aquatic Creatures

While your exploration of foraging has led you through the rich world of aquatic plants, the bounties of water bodies do not stop there. The same environments that foster cattails, wild rice, duckweed, and seaweeds also present another fascinating facet of foraging - the realm of aquatic creatures. Dipping your toes further into the water, you will find a world teeming with shellfish and crustaceans, offering not only sustenance but also an adventurous challenge.

When foraging for aquatic creatures such as clams, mussels, and crabs, timing is of the essence. These creatures are best foraged during low tide when the receding water reveals the seabed and exposes their habitats. Tides follow a regular rhythm, usually with two high tides and two low tides daily. Tide charts, readily available online for most coastal regions, can help you anticipate the best time to go foraging. Once the timing is right, you can follow these strategies for foraging aquatic creatures, specifically clams and crabs.

Digging for Clams

Clams are one of the most coveted prizes for the coastal forager. These bivalve mollusks dwell in the sand or mud at varying depths.

To forage for clams, you'll need to look for "shows" or signs of their presence. These could be small holes or indents in the sand or a jet of water spurting out as the clam retracts its siphon. Once you spot a show, you can dig into the sand with a shovel or your hands to retrieve the clam. Make sure to dig carefully to avoid damaging the clam's delicate shell.

Commonly foraged clams include razor clams, littleneck clams, and quahogs. Each species has its own distinct flavor and texture, making them a diverse addition to your foraging basket.

Catching Crabs

Crab foraging, or crabbing, is a bit more challenging but equally rewarding. Crabs are often found in rocky areas, under seaweed, or in sand or mud burrows during low tide.

Catching crabs requires a cautious approach as they can pinch if they feel threatened. A pair of sturdy gloves can provide some level of protection. Some foragers use crab lines or nets, but you can also catch crabs by hand if you're careful.

Commonly foraged crabs include blue crabs, Dungeness crabs, and stone crabs. Each offers a unique flavor and can be used in a variety of dishes, from crab cakes to rich seafood stews.

Finding drinking water

From the leafy greens of aquatic plants to the delicate shellfish and crustaceans, bodies of water can be a source of nutritious meals. But let's not forget the most vital resource that these habitats provide - water itself. Beyond their abundant flora and fauna, lakes, rivers, and even swamps can become critical lifelines when you find yourself parched during a foraging expedition or in a survival scenario.

Locating water in the wild is just one part of the equation. Gathering it safely and effectively, then purifying it for consumption completes the process. Water is life, and knowing how to obtain safe drinkable water is essential skill for everyone.

Basic Guidelines for Locating Water Sources

However, locating water sources in the wild isn't as simple as finding a lake or a river and drinking straight from it. There are guidelines to follow and dangers to avoid to ensure that the water you consume won't cause more harm than good. The following tips will help steer you in the right direction.

- **Follow Animal Tracks.** Animals need water too, and their well-trodden paths often lead to reliable water sources. Look for converging animal tracks or flying birds during the early morning or late evening - they could be heading to or from a water source.
- **Look for Lush Vegetation.** In arid environments, areas of green, lush vegetation often indicate the presence of water nearby. Be it a hidden stream or an underground source feeding the roots, where plants thrive, water is usually not far.
- **Use Your Ears.** The sound of running water from a stream or a river can often be heard from a distance, especially in quiet, outdoor settings. If you think you hear water, trust your instincts and follow the sound.
- **Check Valleys and Low Areas.** Water naturally flows downhill, collecting in valleys, ditches, or other low areas. If you're in hilly or mountainous terrain, heading downhill can often lead you to a water source.
- **Look to the Sky.** In coastal areas, flocks of birds often fly toward fresh water in the morning and return to the coast at night. Following their direction could lead you to a water source.
- **Observe Insects.** Certain insects, such as mosquitoes, bees, and ants, are generally found within a few hundred

feet of water. While they can be a nuisance, their presence could hint at a nearby water source.

Determining Water Safety

No matter where you find it, water in the wild must be assumed to be unsafe until treated. Harmful pathogens, heavy metals, and chemicals invisible to the naked eye can lurk within, posing serious health risks. While purification methods can help to make it safe to drink, here are a few ways to assess the relative safety of water sources:

Clear is Better. Clear water is always preferable to cloudy or murky water. While clear water can still contain harmful substances, it generally indicates fewer particulates and potential pathogens than its cloudier counterpart.

- **Running Water is Safer.** Streams and rivers tend to be safer than stagnant water bodies like ponds or lakes. The movement of water can help to reduce the concentration of pathogens, though it does not guarantee safety.
- **Check the Source.** If possible, trace the water to its source. A spring bubbling up from the ground is generally cleaner than a river downstream, where it may have picked up contaminants.
- **Presence of Life.** A good sign of relatively safe water is the presence of life. If you see animals drinking from it or aquatic life within it, it is often a safer bet. However, this doesn't guarantee that the water is safe for humans to consume without treatment. Take note if plants surrounding the water source appear unhealthy or discolored, as it could indicate contamination.
- **Smell and Taste.** If the water smells or tastes odd, it might be contaminated. Chemical pollutants often impart an unnatural smell or taste. However, many harmful bacteria

and viruses are odorless and tasteless, so this method is not foolproof.

Remember, these are only initial assessments. Any water sourced in the wild should be purified before consumption to ensure its safety. Read on to learn strategies to help you gather and purify water for drinking.

Gathering and Purifying Water

Once you've located a water source using your foraging skills, the next steps are gathering and purification. Even the clearest mountain stream or spring can contain harmful bacteria, viruses, and parasites. In the following section, I'll cover basic techniques for collecting water from various sources and simple methods for making it safe to drink.

Water Gathering Techniques

Depending on the environment, water may be abundant or scarce. Your methods of collecting it will change accordingly. Here are a few general techniques:

- **Surface water.** Rivers, lakes, and ponds are common sources of water, but they can be contaminated with bacteria, viruses, and other pollutants. It's better to gather water from flowing sources like rivers or streams rather than stagnant ones like ponds or lakes.
- **Rainwater.** Collecting rainwater is a relatively safe way to gather water, especially in rural or wilderness areas. This can be done by spreading out a clean tarp or plastic sheet with a low point in the center to direct the water into a container. However, in urban areas, rainwater may contain pollutants from the atmosphere, so it should be purified before drinking.

- **Dew.** You can gather dew from the grass and leaves early in the morning before the sun evaporates it. This can be done by tying absorbent cloth or a bandana around your ankles and, walking through grassy areas, then wringing out the collected water. While this is a safe source of water, it's also labor-intensive as the amount of water collected is usually small.
- **Transpiration bags.** This is a survival technique to gather water from plants. By tying a clear plastic bag around a leafy branch, the plant's transpiration (release of water) will accumulate as condensation inside the bag. Make sure to use non-toxic plants, and avoid using this method on plants that are under stress, as they may release harmful compounds into the water. The water should be collected by the end of the day when the temperature starts to drop since the decrease in temperature reduces the rate of transpiration.
- **Natural Springs.** Springs are a good source of fresh water, but their quality can vary based on the cleanliness of the source. Do note that even if the water looks clean, it can still contain harmful microorganisms. Therefore, spring water should also be treated before drinking.

Water Purification Methods

Once collected, the water must be purified to remove any harmful pathogens. Here are a few of the most common purification methods:

- **Boiling.** Boiling is one of the most effective methods of purifying water. By bringing water to a rolling boil and maintaining it for at least one minute, most pathogens, such as bacteria, viruses, and parasites, can be killed. Boiling also requires no special equipment, making it a convenient option. However, it does not remove chemicals or heavy metals or improve the taste. It's also worth noting that at higher altitudes, you should boil water for longer since water boils at a lower temperature the higher you go.

- **Water Purification Tablets.** These tablets use chemicals (commonly chlorine, iodine, or chlorine dioxide) to kill bacteria, viruses, and cysts in water. They're lightweight, portable, and relatively easy to use. However, they do have a waiting period (usually 30 minutes to 4 hours) to allow the chemicals to work. Some people also find the taste of the water after treatment unpleasant, but this can often be improved by adding a neutralizer that comes with the tablets or allowing the water to stand open to the air after treatment.
- **Water Filters.** Portable water filters are very useful for outdoor activities or survival situations. They work by forcing water through small pores that remove bacteria, protozoa, and sometimes microplastics. Some high-end models can also filter out some viruses and chemicals. However, filters require manual pumping or gravity feed and they can become clogged, requiring backflushing or replacement of the filter component.
- **UV Light.** Portable UV purifiers use ultraviolet light to kill bacteria, viruses, and protozoa. These are battery-operated devices that are easy to carry and work quickly, usually in less than a minute. However, the water needs to be relatively clear for the UV light to be effective, so pre-filtering might be required. Also, they rely on batteries, so they might not be the best long-term solution.
- **Distillation.** Distillation is the process of boiling water and then collecting the steam. When the steam cools and condenses, it turns back into water, leaving behind most contaminants, including salts and heavy metals. This is one of the few methods that can effectively remove chemical contaminants. However, distillation is energy-intensive and requires more complex equipment than the other methods. In survival situations, it can be challenging

to set up, but in more controlled circumstances, it's an excellent way to purify water.

Do note that no method is 100% effective in all situations, and some methods are better suited for specific contaminants. Therefore, in some cases, combining methods (like filtering and then boiling) might be the safest approach.

Exercise: Survive the Wilderness

In this activity, I'll be challenging you to use your knowledge and skills in an imagined wilderness survival scenario. You will need to find and purify water, considering your resources and potential dangers in the environment.

Scenario:
Imagine you're hiking in a dense forest and suddenly realize you're lost. You have limited supplies: a small multi-tool kit, a plastic water bottle, a piece of cloth, and a waterproof notebook with a pen. You also have a small fire starter. You don't know when you'll be able to find your way back or when help will arrive. You need to find a water source and purify the water for drinking.

Instructions:

1. **Identify Potential Water Sources.** Using your knowledge of foraging, write down in the notebook where you could potentially find water in the environment around you. Remember, water could be found in rivers, streams, lakes, collected rainwater, dew on plants, and even in certain types of plants or trees themselves.
2. **Analyze Each Source.** Now consider each source and write down potential risks and benefits. Think about the cleanliness of the water, the dangers in reaching it, and what tools you have at your disposal.

3. **Choose Your Source.** Decide on the most suitable source. Write down your reasoning for this choice.
4. **Collect the Water.** Describe how you would use your available tools to collect the water. Would you use your bottle directly? Would you use the cloth to soak up dew?
5. **Purify the Water.** Next, detail how you would purify the water with your limited tools. You could use the fire starter to boil the water if you have a container that can handle the heat. Or, you might use the cloth as a rudimentary filter.
6. **Consider the Risks.** Finally, consider potential risks or errors in your plan. For example, is the fire starter reliable? Could the cloth have contaminants? How would you mitigate these risks?

Analysis:
After you have completed your written survival plan, take some time to review and analyze it. The goal is to reinforce what you've learned, identify any areas of improvement, and consider other potential strategies. Use the following points to guide your analysis:

- Look at the list of potential water sources you came up with. Did you consider all the possible sources of water in the environment you described? Reflect on any sources you might have missed and why.
- Reflect on the potential risks and benefits you listed for each water source. Were your assessments realistic, or did you perhaps overlook any crucial factors, such as the potential for pollution or the difficulty of accessing the source?
- Reconsider the water source you chose. Was it the most practical and safe choice, given your situation and the tools at hand? Could there have been a better choice?
- Look at the method you chose to collect the water. Was it the most effective and safe method using the tools you had? If not, what other method could you have used?

- Review your water purification plan. Would the method you chose effectively purify the water? Were there potential risks or errors in your plan?
- Reflect on the potential risks or errors in your overall plan. How might these risks impact your survival in this scenario, and how could you modify your plan to mitigate them?

Remember, the goal isn't to be perfect but to learn and grow from the activity. This is a valuable opportunity to critically think about the skills of water foraging and purification and how you could apply them in a real-life scenario.

Chapter 7
Environment-Specific Foraging

In the vast and diverse world of foraging, every environment is a new opportunity. From the deep, verdant expanse of forests and woodlands to the saline touch of coastal regions, and even in the heart of our urban landscapes, nature offers an astonishing variety of edible gifts.

The realm of foraging is far-reaching, extending beyond rural and wild spaces and surprisingly plunging into the heart of cities. Each of these environments presents unique offerings and distinct challenges that will be explored in depth. I will also share the diverse species available in these specific environments, focusing on the most common ones you will likely encounter on your foraging journey.

I will also touch on those species to be cautious of or avoid entirely, highlighting not only the delights but also the potential dangers that lie within natural and urban landscapes. Lastly, I also include additional equipment you may need aside from those I mentioned previously on the forager's toolkit. So, whether you're venturing into the woods, walking along the beach, or wandering through city parks and alleyways, this chapter will equip you with the knowledge and guidance needed to navigate these environments with the confidence and curiosity of a seasoned forager.

Forests and Woodlands

The lush canopy of the world's forests and woodlands is rich and diverse. These environments provide an abundance of resources, from the sweet, hidden berries to the towering trees bearing nuts and other delights. Foraging in forests and woodlands can be a gratifying experience, connecting you to our ancestors who relied on these resources for survival.

Forests and woodlands are characterized by different animal and plant species that form a complex and interwoven web of life. While forests typically denote a denser, more closed canopy, woodlands are characterized by more open spaces, allowing sunlight to reach the undergrowth and support a greater diversity of plants.

The seasonal changes greatly impact foraging opportunities in these environments. For instance, the arrival of spring brings with it an explosion of growth and the emergence of certain species, such as wild garlic and morels, while autumn provides an array of nuts and fruits.

Common Edible Species

Listed below are species you could expect to see in forests and woodlands.

Trees

Forests are home to a wide variety of towering trees, each offering resources you can forage. For instance, the stately Oak, in addition to providing shelter and shade, bestows a bounty of acorns each autumn. When properly leached to remove their bitter tannins, acorns can be ground into flour, offering a gluten-free alternative for baking.

Birch trees, with their distinctive white bark, are another generous provider. In early spring, their sap can be tapped to yield a refreshing drink rich in minerals and vitamins. When reduced, it transforms into a deliciously sweet syrup, perfect for drizzling over pancakes or using in marinades.

Fruit and nut trees add further variety. Wild apple trees, bearing fruits that range from tart to sweet, can offer a satisfying snack during a foraging hike. Hazelnut trees, distinguished by their round, fringed husks, yield protein-rich nuts that are perfect for a quick energy boost.

Shrubs and Bushes

Shrubs and bushes are nature's candy stores as they offer sweet berries. The trailing vines of the blackberry bush, for example, bear clusters of juicy fruits, bursting with sweet-tart flavor. These berries can be eaten fresh or used in various culinary creations, from pies to preserves.

Hawthorn bushes, usually seen near woods or in hedges, provide food in autumn. Their berries, or haws, are perfect for making heart-warming jellies and syrups. While the seeds are not edible, the flesh of the haw is rich in antioxidants and can offer a tangy punch to autumn dishes.

Understory Plants

The understory, the area under the trees and covered by leaves, is home to a range of aromatic, flavorful plants. Wild garlic, or "ramsons," is one such treasure. Emerging in early spring, it blankets the forest floor with its wide, green leaves and star-like white flowers. The leaves can be used like conventional garlic but offer a milder flavor, making them perfect for pesto, salads, and infused oils.

Also, part of the understory's treasures are ramps or wild leeks. Resembling a scallion, ramps have broad, flat leaves that give way to a small white bulb. Both leaves and bulb are edible, possessing a potent flavor that combines the punch of onion and the zest of garlic. They're a wonderful addition to soups, stir-fries, and egg dishes, providing a hint of wildness to any meal.

Foraging Equipment and Safety Measures

When foraging in forests and woodlands, the following clothing and equipment are recommended:

Clothing

- **Lightweight, durable, and long-sleeved clothing:** Offers protection from thorns, insects, and potential irritants.
- **Breathable fabrics:** Provides comfort during lengthy foraging sessions.
- **Waterproof boots:** Essential for keeping feet dry in wet or damp conditions.
- **Hat:** Protects against the sun and falling debris.
- **Bright colors:** Increases visibility, particularly during hunting seasons.

Equipment:

- **Tarp:** This can be useful for collecting nuts or fruits that are falling from trees. Simply spread it on the ground to catch the falling bounty.
- **Insect Repellent:** Protect yourself from mosquito bites and ticks which are common in woodland areas.
- **Headlamp or flashlight:** These are essential if you're foraging around dawn or dusk, especially in dense forest areas where light can be limited.

- **Binoculars:** Helps spot high-up tree fruits or nests.
- **Sturdy walking stick:** Assists in difficult terrains and can be used to disturb the undergrowth for creature checks.
- **Sharp knife:** Useful for harvesting plants and fungi.

Anticipated Obstacles and Threats

Foraging in forests and woodlands, while an enriching experience, does pose certain challenges and potential dangers.

Firstly, the *dense and expansive nature of these environments can make it easy to lose your bearings.* This could potentially result in getting lost, which can be dangerous without proper navigation tools or skills.

Secondly, *these areas are home to a variety of wildlife, some of which may pose a threat to humans.* From venomous snakes to large mammals like bears or mountain lions, it's essential to be aware of the potential wildlife encounters in your foraging area and know how to respond appropriately. Ticks and other insects are another concern in wooded areas, as they can transmit diseases such as Lyme disease. Wearing appropriate clothing and using insect repellents can help protect against these.

Another risk is a wide array of *poisonous plants and fungi.* Misidentification can have serious consequences, so thorough knowledge and careful identification are crucial.

Lastly, the *forest environment can be physically challenging with rough terrains and unexpected weather changes.* It's always a good idea to check the weather forecast, inform someone about your foraging plans, and be prepared with suitable clothing and equipment.

Coastal Regions

Coastal areas are usually located by the sea, providing a unique landscape where the water meets the land. The sea breeze, the sound of waves, and the salty air make these regions distinctive. They're home to diverse plants and wildlife, including seagrasses, sea herbs, shellfish, and seaweed. The sandy or rocky terrain, varying temperatures, and tidal changes all contribute to a different foraging experience compared to forests or fields.

Common Edible Species

The coastal landscape is rich in edible species. Let's explore some of the most common and palatable.

Sea Vegetables

Coastlines provide an array of sea vegetables that are highly nutritious and offer a taste of the ocean. Kelp, a type of large brown seaweed, is rich in iodine and can be used in soups, salads, or even as a wrap for sushi.

Sea lettuce, a delicate green seaweed, grows in shallow water and can be eaten raw or lightly steamed. It's a great addition to salads and sandwiches, lending a subtly salty flavor.

Dulse, a reddish-purple seaweed, is another marine delight that can be eaten raw or cooked. It has a slightly spicy flavor and is often used in soups, stews, and stir-fry.

Shellfish

Coastal regions are a shellfish forager's dream. The mudflats and shallow waters are home to a plethora of bivalves. Clams, identified by their rounded or oval shell, are a nutritious source of protein and can be steamed, fried, or used in chowders.

Mussels, with their distinctive blue-black shells, cling to rocky shorelines and pilings. They're deliciously steamed in a garlic and white wine broth or incorporated into pasta dishes.

Oysters, although requiring a bit more effort to forage and open, are a delicacy. Enjoy them raw, grilled, or baked with a splash of lemon juice.

Foraging Equipment

When foraging in coastal regions, the following clothing and equipment are suggested:

Clothing

- **Wind-resistant jacket:** Protects against coastal breezes.
- **Waterproof clothing:** Useful for foraging at low tide and handling wet seaweed and shellfish.
- **Sun protection:** Hat, sunglasses, and sunscreen to shield against intense coastal sun.
- **Sturdy water shoes:** Provides protection against sharp rocks and shells and provides grip on slippery surfaces.

Equipment

- **Tide Table:** Crucial for planning safe and productive foraging around tide schedules.
- **Oyster knife or other sturdy picks:** Necessary for shellfish harvesting.
- **Fishing net or rod:** If you plan to catch small fish or shrimps.
- **Plastic trays or boxes:** Useful for sorting and transporting delicate finds such as shellfish.

Safety in coastal regions involves being aware of the tide and never turning your back on the sea. Coastal foraging is greatly influenced by the ocean's conditions, so it's vital to check local weather and tide forecasts before heading out.

Anticipated Obstacles and Threats

Coastal foraging presents its unique set of challenges. The most immediate is the *changing tides*. These can shift incredibly fast, potentially trapping the unwary forager on isolated patches of the beach. Always be aware of the tide times and stay vigilant.

Weather conditions at the coast can change rapidly, and a clear sky can quickly turn stormy. The coastline is often *a windy place*, and this can make conditions feel colder than they are, leading to the risk of hypothermia if not adequately clothed.

Additionally, some coastal areas may be *home to potentially dangerous wildlife,* from stinging jellyfish to territorial sea birds. It's essential to respect wildlife and keep a safe distance.

Finally, while many coastal species are edible, some can be *harmful if not prepared correctly*. Shellfish, for example, can cause severe food poisoning if not cooked thoroughly.

Urban Landscapes

Urban landscapes may not seem like the ideal foraging grounds, but you'll be surprised at the number of edible species that thrive in the heart of our cities. Parks, vacant lots, and even sidewalk cracks can host a range of edible plants and fungi. Urban foraging allows you to connect with nature within your concrete jungles and fosters a sense of self-sufficiency.

Common Edible Species

Cities hide edible treasures in plain sight. Here are some species that are common in urban environments.

Weeds and Trees

Amid the urban sprawl, a host of edible species thrive. Common weeds, often ignored or despised, are a readily available resource. Dandelions, with their bright yellow flowers, can be found in lawns and parks. Their leaves make a nutritious addition to salads, while their roots can be used to make a coffee substitute.

Purslane, a succulent weed, sprouts in cracks in sidewalks and driveways. It's rich in omega-3 fatty acids and can be eaten raw or cooked.

Like in forests, trees play a significant role in urban foraging. Urban trees, such as mulberries and black walnuts, produce fruits and nuts that can be collected in the summer and autumn months. Their size may not rival their woodland counterparts, but they offer the urban forager a rich bounty.

Berries and Herbs

Fruit-bearing shrubs, such as blackberries and raspberries, can often be found in urban green spaces, along walking trails, and in overgrown lots. Their juicy fruits are perfect for snacking, baking, or jam-making.

Many herbs also flourish in the city. Mint, with its refreshing aroma, often grows wild in moist, shady spots. Rosemary can be found in urban gardens and public landscaping. Fennel, with its feathery leaves and aniseed flavor, is a common sight in many city parks. These herbs can add a punch of flavor to your urban-foraged meals.

Foraging Equipment

When foraging in urban landscapes, the following clothing and equipment are recommended:

Clothing

- **Comfortable, sturdy shoes:** Urban environments often require much walking on concrete.
- **Gloves:** To protect hands from dirt, sharp objects, and potential pollutants.
- **Casual and comfortable clothing:** Suitable for the urban setting and the potential for variable weather.

Equipment

- **Small pruning shears:** Useful for harvesting in tight spaces or thick growths.
- **Hygiene products:** Hand sanitizer or wipes for cleaning hands before and after foraging.
- **Pollution map**: Urban areas may have zones of high pollution. It's a good idea to avoid foraging in these areas.

Anticipated Obstacles and Threats

In the concrete jungles, urban foragers face a different range of challenges. One of the primary concerns is *pollution*. Plants near busy roads can absorb harmful pollutants, and those in industrial areas may be exposed to chemical contamination. Therefore, you must choose your foraging spots wisely and avoid areas of heavy traffic or industrial activity.

Secondly, you also need to have a thorough *understanding of public and private boundaries in the city*. It's illegal and unethical to forage on private property without permission, and certain public areas may have restrictions too. Always respect these boundaries.

Another possible concern in urban areas is the *presence of pests*. Rats and other urban wildlife can carry diseases, so always ensure to wash your finds thoroughly.

And just as in any environment, *species misidentification* can lead to serious consequences. Many ornamental plants used in urban landscaping are non-native and potentially toxic. Urban foragers must be knowledgeable about these plants and always be certain of a plant's identity before consuming it.

Exercise: Foraging Scavenger Hunt

This exercise is designed to enhance your foraging skills by encouraging you to identify and learn about different edible species in various environments. Whether you're exploring forests, combing coastal regions, or navigating urban landscapes, this activity will emphasize the importance of observing the environment, as different species have specific habitats and growing conditions. It's also a fun way to compare the richness and diversity of edible species in different environments.

Instructions:

1. **Research:** Begin by researching common edible species found in your region during the current season. Be sure to look for species specific to the environment you will be exploring (forest, coast, or urban). Make a list of these species and gather detailed information about their identifying features, habitats, and any look-alikes to avoid.
2. **Prepare:** Create a scavenger hunt list that includes a range of species across different categories. For example, you

could include a variety of trees, bushes, ground plants, and fungi if you're foraging in a forest or woodland. If you're in an urban area, the list may include common weeds, tree fruits, and herbs. For coastal regions, consider seaweed, shellfish, and coastal plants.
3. **Explore:** Set out on your foraging adventure. Use your list to guide your search. Try to find and identify as many species on your list as possible. Don't forget to bring along a field guide or use a reliable plant identification app to help you.
4. **Document:** Take photos or sketch the species you find. Note down their characteristics and the habitat in which you found them. This can serve as a personal foraging guide over time.
5. **Reflect and Compare:** After your hunt, review the species you found and those you didn't. Research more about the species on your list, especially those that you were unable to identify. If you've completed the scavenger hunt in different environments, compare your findings. What species were common across all environments? Which were unique to each environment?
6. **Repeat:** Keep practicing. You can do the scavenger hunt regularly, changing the species on your list according to the seasons. Try the hunt in different environments to learn about the diverse array of edibles each one has to offer.

Remember, the goal isn't just to collect and consume the species you find (although you certainly can, with proper identification and ethical practices). The primary aim is to improve your identification skills, broaden your knowledge, and deepen your understanding and appreciation of nature's bounty in diverse settings. As your confidence grows, you'll be able to apply these skills to harvest and enjoy a wider range of wild foods safely and sustainably.

Chapter 8
Sustainable Foraging

Sustainable foraging is more than simply wandering through the woods, plucking wild berries from bushes, or digging up earthy tubers from beneath the leaf litter. It's a thoughtful, purposeful activity that ensures the ecosystems you engage with are as healthy and vibrant after you've passed through as they were before.

You might be asking, "Why is this so important?" After all, Mother Nature is bountiful, right? Indeed, she is! But you live in a world where natural resources are finite. They are now under pressure, and every action you take can tip the balance, no matter how small. So, when you forage sustainably, you're not just harvesting food; you're nurturing the land that nurtures you.

Imagine you're walking through a sun-dappled forest, where the trunks of tall, majestic trees reach up to meet a clear blue sky. A variety of ferns brush against your legs, and a light breeze carries the sweet scent of blooming flowers. You spot a patch of wild strawberries, their bright red fruits winking at you from the greenery. If you're a sustainable forager, you'd take a few ripe strawberries for yourself and leave the rest for the local wildlife and other foragers.

But consider another scenario. Suppose you come across a rare, edible mushroom species growing near an old, fallen log. A traditional forager might scoop up every single one of them without a second thought. But in doing so, they're reducing the chances of that mushroom species regrowing in the same area.

Whenever you step into the great outdoors, you interact with the ecosystem. Like a pebble thrown into a pond, your actions send ripples through the environment. The same is true for foraging. But is this impact beneficial or harmful? Or can it be both? Let's take a closer look.

Why Sustainable Foraging Matters

Sustainable foraging – if done right – can be like a gentle hand caressing the pond's surface. It brings benefits not just to the forager but to the ecosystem as well.

One benefit lies in *spreading plant species*. Think of picking blackberries, for instance. Each blackberry is a tiny package of seeds. After you've enjoyed your blackberry pie or jam, the seeds often end up back in nature through composting or even natural processes. This contributes to the natural spread and propagation of the blackberry bush.

Another advantage is the *control of invasive species*. In many regions, invasive plants grow rampantly, crowding out native flora and disrupting ecosystems. By identifying, harvesting, and eating these intruders, foragers can help control their spread. Japanese Knotweed, for example, is an invasive species in North America and Europe. But did you know it's also edible when young and can be cooked similarly to rhubarb? Foragers can thus become allies in ecological conservation efforts.

Thirdly, sustainable foraging can also lead to *heightened ecological awareness*. A conscientious forager is an observer of the natural world, gaining an understanding of the rhythms of plant and animal life. He develops a personal stake in the health of the environment. This can translate into more significant involvement in conservation initiatives, promoting biodiversity, and advocating for the protection of natural habitats.

Potential Negative Consequences of Over-foraging

Unfortunately, not all ripples caused by foraging are positive. When the practice tips into over-foraging, those gentle ripples can become disruptive waves, causing harm to the ecosystem.

One negative impact of over-foraging is the *potential depletion of plant species*. A prime example is the wild ginseng root in North America, which has been excessively harvested to the point of being declared endangered in some regions. When a plant species is over-foraged, it doesn't just affect that single species; it can disrupt the entire food chain.

In some cases, foraging can lead to *habitat destruction*. Trampling vegetation, compacting soil, and leaving litter can damage habitats and make them less hospitable for plants and wildlife. Even off-trail hiking in search of wild edibles can contribute to erosion and disturb sensitive species.

Finally, over-foraging can contribute to the *spread of diseases and pests*. Disturbing plants or digging in the soil can unintentionally spread pathogens or insects that harm plant health. One example is the spread of Phytophthora ramorum, a plant pathogen causing devastating diseases in forests and landscapes, which can be transmitted through soil stuck on foragers' shoes.

So, is foraging a friend or foe to ecosystems? The answer isn't a definite black and white. The impact largely depends on how you forage. There lies the delicate balance. Done responsibly, foraging can be a way of connecting with nature that's beneficial to both you and the environment. However, over-foraging can lead to serious ecological consequences. It's a reminder that the privilege of enjoying nature's bounty comes with the responsibility of ensuring its survival for generations to come.

Principles of Ethical Foraging

Like every venture into the natural world, foraging comes with responsibilities. Ethical foraging is akin to an unspoken agreement between you and the natural world: you are permitted to take its bounty, but you must also act as its guardian. Remember, foraging ethically isn't just about ensuring there will be plants to harvest next season. It's about maintaining biodiversity, supporting ecosystem health, and respecting the interconnections between all living things.

- **Do take only what you need.** This principle reminds you to harvest with moderation. Your instinct might be to gather all the delicious berries you can find, but you have to remember that these resources are not unlimited. Overharvesting can cause a decline in plant populations and even lead to the extinction of certain species in the area. Additionally, many animals rely on these resources for their survival. By only taking what you need, you're ensuring that there will be plenty left for wildlife and for future generations of foragers.
- **Do tread lightly.** As foragers, you must strive to minimize your impact on the environment. This means being mindful of where you step to avoid crushing plants or disturbing habitats. It also includes packing out any trash or other materials you bring with you.
- **Don't take rare species.** If you come across a plant or mushroom that doesn't seem to be abundant in the area, it's best to leave it alone. These organisms might be struggling to maintain their populations, and even minor disruptions could have significant impacts. If you're unsure about a species' status, it's better to err on the side of caution and leave it untouched.

The essence of these principles revolves around one fundamental idea: **respect**. Respect for the wildlife you share these spaces with, respect for the ecosystems that sustain them, and respect for the balance that exists between us all. Once you adhere to these principles, you can ensure your foraging practice is genuinely sustainable, not only concerning the plants you harvest but also in your interactions with the wider ecosystem.

Understanding Foraging Laws

Following on from your exploration of the principles of sustainable foraging, you also have to touch upon another cornerstone of this practice - understanding and adhering to the laws that govern foraging activities.

Foraging laws are complex and vary widely across different regions and countries, influenced by a myriad of factors such as property rights, conservation concerns, and local customs. Here, you'll dive into some general aspects of these laws to provide a foundational understanding for budding foragers.

Respecting Land Ownership

Firstly, knowing who owns the land you plan to forage on is essential. Private land is subject to the ownership rights of the individual or organization that holds it. That means if you wish to forage on private land, you must seek permission from the landowner. In some cases, landowners may grant foraging rights, possibly for a fee, while others may strictly forbid it.

On public lands like national parks, forests, or local green spaces, foraging is generally allowed but often with restrictions. These restrictions can limit the types and quantities of species you can harvest and sometimes even the methods of harvesting.

Knowing Local Customs

Local customs can play a significant role in foraging laws. This is particularly true in regions where foraging is tied to historical or cultural practices. For example, in Sweden, the right to roam, or 'allemansrätten', allows everyone to forage freely on both private and public lands, provided they do not disturb or destroy the environment or private property. However, this isn't the case everywhere. In many parts of the U.S., for example, regulations vary from state to state and even from one park or forest to another. Make sure to check local regulations before setting off on your foraging expedition.

Being Aware of Conservation Rights

In addition to land ownership and local customs, another significant factor to consider when foraging is conservation laws. These laws are designed to protect native plant and animal species, maintaining the health and diversity of ecosystems and avoiding any harmful effects that might come from overharvesting.

The Endangered Species Act in the United States, for example, prohibits the collection of any species listed as threatened or endangered. This includes plants and animals alike, many of which are crucial to the health of their ecosystems. Picking a plant that's listed as endangered, even if you didn't know it was, could result in heavy penalties.

Most regions have similar restrictions on the harvesting of protected species. This information can usually be found on government websites or by consulting local conservationists or park rangers.

Moreover, some conservation laws regulate not only what you can forage but also when and how. For instance, there may be limits on the quantities of certain species that can be harvested in a given period or restrictions on the use of certain tools that can damage plants or their habitats. Some places may prohibit foraging altogether during certain times of the year to allow plant species to reproduce or recover.

Practicing Conservation and Rehabilitation

As you delve deeper into the intriguing world of foraging and learn more about its associated laws and regulations, it's paramount to recognize the responsibilities that come along with this enriching activity. Today, you journey into the heart of foraging responsibility, focusing on forage conservation and rehabilitation. This is the point where the law meets environmental stewardship, where each of us, as part of the global foraging community, can make a meaningful impact.

Let's explore this essential aspect of foraging, discussing how to promote conservation, rehabilitate over-foraged areas, and how community involvement can make a difference.

Promoting Conservation in Foraging Areas

When foraging, it's not merely about harvesting from the wild but forming a symbiotic relationship with nature. This relationship requires keen attention to conservation. Here are several ways you can achieve this:

- **Practice Ethical Foraging.** As discussed earlier, this means only taking what you need and leaving enough for the plants to reproduce and for wildlife to feed on. By doing so, you help maintain the balance of the ecosystem and allow it to continue to thrive.
- **Record Your Findings:** Document your foraging activities and report your findings to local environmental or

conservation groups. This citizen science can be helpful in monitoring local species and their growth patterns.
- **Be a Role Model:** Set a good example for others by following all the best practices of foraging. Show respect for nature and share your commitment to conservation with others. Your responsible behavior can inspire others to do the same.
- **Abiding by Marine Foraging Laws.** Marine foraging, like clam digging or seaweed harvesting, also has specific laws and regulations. These are often designed to protect marine ecosystems and ensure the sustainability of marine species. Before heading to the beach, make sure to acquaint yourself with local laws, which may include restrictions on size, species, and season.
- **Active Participation in Conservation.** Foragers can help by reporting issues like illegal dumping, suspicious activities in foraging areas, or potential threats to protected areas. For example, if you notice an area where litter is becoming a problem, you could organize a cleanup. If you spot a rare or endangered species, report it to local conservation authorities.
- **Education and Awareness.** Share your knowledge about sustainable foraging practices and the importance of conservation with friends, family, and your local community. This could be through informal conversations or more structured activities like workshops or guided foraging walks.

Rehabilitation of Over-foraged Areas

Sadly, over-foraging can lead to areas becoming depleted and habitats being damaged. In these cases, active rehabilitation may be necessary to help nature recover.

Replanting is one of the most obvious steps in rehabilitating over-foraged areas. This doesn't mean just planting anything, though. The goal is to restore the area as close as possible to its original state. That means choosing native species and ensuring they're suitable for the specific conditions of the area.

Consider planting seeds, cuttings, or young plants and aim to mimic nature. For instance, instead of planting in neat rows as you would in a garden, scatter seeds randomly to create a more natural effect.

But plants aren't the only focus. Remember also to *consider the wildlife that depends on these plants.* For example, if an area has been stripped of berry bushes, not only has the plant population suffered, but the birds that rely on those berries have too. When you replant the berry bushes, you're helping both the plants and the wildlife.

Nurturing growth is also essential. Monitor the area regularly, water if necessary, and keep an eye out for threats like disease, pests, or further over-foraging. This nurturing period is crucial as the young plants establish themselves and begin to regenerate the area.

Citizen Science and Community Involvement in Forage Conservation

The conservation of our natural spaces is a massive task, and it's one that we can all contribute to, particularly through citizen science and community involvement.

Citizen science is a way for ordinary people to contribute to scientific research. This could be through observing and recording plant populations, noting the timing of seasonal changes (phenology), or reporting sightings of specific species. Many conservation organizations and universities run citizen science projects and are often eager for foragers to get involved. Your observations while out foraging can contribute valuable data to these projects.

Community involvement is another powerful tool for conservation. There's strength in numbers, and when a community comes together to protect and manage their local foraging areas, real change can happen. This could be through forming a local foraging group to promote sustainable practices, hosting educational events, or organizing conservation activities like clean-ups or replanting days. Involving the community in conservation not only benefits nature but can also strengthen the community itself. Working together towards a shared goal can build relationships, foster a sense of pride in the local area, and even improve community health and well-being.

Schools can also be a part of this. Encouraging these to include foraging and conservation in their curriculum can foster a love of nature in the next generation and teach them the importance of protecting it. After all, today's young foragers are tomorrow's conservation leaders.

Interacting with Wildlife

As a forager, your exploration stretches far beyond the vegetation and fungi, extending into the lively domain of the creatures who inhabit these natural spaces. Thus, engaging with wildlife ethically and responsibly is integral to sustainable foraging, ensuring you contribute positively to the ecosystems you visit and do not disrupt the natural balance.

Each step you take in the wild places you forage at is an entry into the homes of countless creatures. These interactions aren't just incidental encounters. They are an important opportunity to learn and appreciate the intricate balance of nature. It's in these moments that you truly understand how interconnected all life forms are and how your actions can influence their well-being and the overall health of their habitats.

Dos and Don'ts of Wildlife Encounters

Respect is at the core of all wildlife encounters. It's about understanding that you are visitors in their habitat and that everything you do can have a lasting impact. Here are some key dos and don'ts to keep in mind when encountering wildlife during your foraging escapades:

- **Do Observe from a Distance.** Wildlife is best admired from afar. Give them plenty of space to go about their natural behaviors undisturbed. This not only respects their needs but also reduces the potential stress that close human interaction can cause.
- **Don't Feed or Attempt to Touch Animals.** As tempting as it might be to extend a friendly hand, feeding wildlife can significantly alter their natural behaviors and diets, leading to long-term harm. Attempting to touch or pet wild animals can provoke defensive behaviors, posing a risk to both you and the animal.
- **Be Quiet and Gentle: Try to blend in with nature.** Walk lightly, talk softly, and move slowly. Startling wildlife can lead to stress responses that can have detrimental effects on their health and survival.
- **Don't Chase or Follow.** Respect the animal's need for space and safety. Chasing or following wildlife can be stressful and scary for them, leading to harmful changes in their behaviors or potentially forcing them into dangerous situations.
- **Do Leave No Trace.** Make sure to carry out anything you bring in. Leaving garbage behind can be harmful to wildlife and the environment.
- **Don't Disturb Nests or Dens.** If you find a nest or a den, stay away from it. Touching it can scare the animals and might make mothers leave their babies. If you are foraging for eggs, the best time to do it is when the mother is not present, to

reduce stress and disturbance. However, be quick and quiet to minimize the chance of the mother abandoning the nest due to perceived threat. But remember, always leave some eggs behind to ensure the future generation of that species.

Conclusion

Foraging has long been a staple survival technique of our ancestors, providing a crucial lifeline to early societies and cultures. Yet, in this era of fast food, supermarkets, and online groceries, people have lost touch with these age-old practices. The journey you've undertaken through this book has hopefully reconnected you to this ancient art and, more importantly, to the natural world around you.

You began your journey by learning the fundamentals of foraging, a complex yet rewarding skill that rekindles your innate connection to the environment. I hope that knowing the basics prepared you for the diverse landscapes you would encounter and the myriad of edible species they host.

Next, you delved into the art of plant identification, a skill fundamental to successful foraging. This knowledge proved invaluable, distinguishing the edible from the poisonous, and allowing you to navigate the bountiful world of plants safely. Recognizing the details of leaf patterns, stem structures, and flowering sequences offered a fresh perspective on the intricate detailing of Mother Nature.

Medicinal plant foraging opened your eyes to the power of nature's pharmacy. These plants, often overlooked, have profound healing properties, and have served as the cornerstone of traditional medicine across cultures. As you journeyed through this section, you discovered the profound wisdom inherent in the natural world, transforming these miraculous and healing plants into different forms such as syrups and balms.

From plants, you shifted your focus to the fungi kingdom, an often underexplored facet of the foraging world. Looking for fungi opened up new possibilities, as there are many different kinds that can be used for food and medicine. Learning about and identifying fungi showed you a magical world that's often out of sight, highlighting the key part fungi play in nature.

Subsequently, I shared with you protein-rich foraging, a vital component for sustenance and survival in the wild. This section highlighted the importance of maintaining a balanced diet, demonstrating that nature offers more than just plant-based food sources but a holistic nutritional palette. It also aimed to help you widen your perspective to not limit your protein sources to meat by foraging insects and eggs.

Water, the elixir of life, was the next focus. Truly, there is more to water than quenching thirst as it gives you other foraging options such as aquatic plants and crustaceans. However, this chapter also showed you that finding safe, drinkable water is not a walk in the park. The ability to locate and purify water will help you prepare to survive in diverse environments.

Then, I shared with you the three most common places you can forage, namely, forest and woodlands, coastal regions and urban landscapes. Here you learned about the most prevalent species to seek out during foraging, along with the necessary equipment and appropriate attire to use according to the specific location of your foraging expedition.

Finally, I tied all these elements together through sustainable and ethical foraging. This section reiterated the importance of respecting nature, harvesting responsibly, and ensuring the continuity of ecosystems for generations to come. You learned that true mastery lies not in exploiting the resources around us but in understanding and nurturing them.

All in all, let the knowledge you gained from this book be not a mere addition to your survival toolkit, but a way of life, a philosophy that shapes your view of the world. Let it inspire respect for the intricate web of life that sustains and an understanding that everything in nature is connected. As you tread the foraging path, remember that each plant you gather, each water source you uncover, each fungus you harvest, plays a crucial role in the larger symphony of life. They all whisper the same truth – that you are a part of the environment, not apart from it.

Nature is not just a provider of food and medicine but a haven for the spirit, a place where you can rejuvenate, reconnect, and rediscover your place in the world. As you forage, you are not merely 'taking'; you are entering a reciprocal relationship with the natural world, a partnership of mutual respect and understanding.

Each step you take on the foraging path leads you closer to the ancient practices of our ancestors, echoing in the rustle of the leaves and the whisper of the wind. You are drawn into an age-old dance, choreographed by the wisdom of the seasons and the cycle of life. Through foraging, you do not only sustain your body but feed your soul, satisfying a primal hunger that modern living often leaves unattended.

However, the knowledge and skills that you have acquired are not merely for your own benefit. They are a legacy to be handed down, seeds to be sown in the minds of future generations. By passing on this wisdom, you ensure that the bond between man and nature endures, that the art of foraging is kept alive. May the respect for the natural world never be lost.

As you close this book, let it not be the end of your journey but a beacon guiding you forward. Each page turned, each chapter read, is a stepping stone on your personal path to discovery and connection. May this knowledge inspire in you a deep reverence for the intricacy and majesty of the natural world.

May the trees be your teachers, their leaves the pages of an unending book, their fruits the rewards of your learning. May the rivers quench your thirst for knowledge, their stream a constant reminder of the flow of life. May the mushrooms and fungi that spring from the earth nourish your curiosity and the insects and small animals that share your path deepen your understanding of the interconnectedness of all living beings.

Let the spirit of foraging guide you towards a more meaningful, mindful, and sustainable way of life. Let it inspire you to protect, conserve, and cherish our natural world. For in doing so, you secure not only your survival but the survival of this beautiful, fragile planet, and all the diverse, incredible life it sustains.

Remember these words and keep them in your heart: "I do not inherit nature, but rather, I borrow it from the generations to come. My actions today are the promises I make for their tomorrow. So, l will walk softly, forage responsibly, and live gratefully."

Techniques Recap

The following techniques are found in "Foraging [All in 1]:

#	Techniques / Hacks	Explanation
1	Keep an Eye on the Skies	Be alert for falling trees or loose branches, particularly in windy conditions or after a storm, as they can be dangerous.
2	Choose Pollution-Free Areas	Opt for spaces untouched by pollution, away from industrial sites and potentially contaminated water bodies, where nature grows freely and safely.
3	Inform Someone About Your Foraging Plans	Always let a friend, family member, or neighbor know about your foraging plans, including your location, route, and estimated return time. Update them if plans change.
4	Berry Identification Caution	Avoid tasting unknown berries unless you're certain of their identification.
5	Recognizing Poisonous Plants	Identify poison ivy, oak, and sumac by their leaf clusters and appearances to avoid contact.
6	Bitter Taste Warning	A bitter taste from plants, like hemlock or parts of elderberry, is a red flag for toxicity.
7	Careful Consumption of Foraged Items	Inspect plants carefully before eating. Don't rush into consumption.
8	Plant Component Separation	Separate and assess each part of the plant as their properties can vary.
9	Lip Test for Plant Safety	Test a small portion of the plant on your lip to check for adverse reactions like burning or itching.
10	Tongue Test for Edibility	Place the plant part on your tongue without swallowing to test for discomfort or adverse reactions.
11	Developing a Foraging Calendar	Observe plant cycles throughout the year in regular natural spaces to create a personalized foraging calendar.
12	Creating Echinacea Tincture	Make echinacea tincture by soaking the plant's roots, leaves, and flowers in alcohol, then straining after six weeks.
13	Making Calendula Salves	Infuse calendula flowers in a carrier oil, then mix with beeswax to make salves for skin ailments.
14	Preparing Elderberries	Simmer elderberries in water, strain, and mix with honey to make an immune-boosting syrup.
15	Capturing Crickets	Find crickets in grassy fields, meadows, gardens, or urban green spaces using a sweep net.

Foraging [All in 1]

#	Techniques / Hacks	Explanation
16	Finding Mealworms	Look for mealworms in dark, damp areas like under logs or in compost.
17	Catching Grasshoppers	Catch protein-dense grasshoppers in grassy fields, especially in the cool early mornings.
18	Gentle Insect Catching	Be patient and gentle when catching insects to avoid startling them.
19	Using Appropriate Tools for Insects	Utilize tools like sweep nets for easier insect catching.
20	Wearing Protective Clothing for Insect Catching	Protect yourself from insect bites or stings by wearing gloves and other protective gear.
21	Purging Insects Before Cooking	Keep captured insects in a ventilated container without food for 24 hours to purge their systems.
22	Boiling Insects for Safety	Boil insects briefly to kill parasites and remove toxins, followed by rinsing.
23	Egg Freshness Test	Test egg freshness by placing it in water; fresh eggs sink, older ones float. Always conduct additional checks for safety.
24	Foraging for Eggs	Look for signs like bird droppings or feathers for nests and disturbed soil or sand for reptile eggs.
25	Making a Mushroom Spore Print	Create a spore print from a mushroom by placing its cap on paper, covering it, and waiting for spores to fall.
26	Avoid Tasting Unknown Plants	Avoid tasting unknown plants due to the risk of toxin ingestion.
27	Caution with Uncertain Aquatic Plants	Avoid direct contact or consumption of aquatic plants if their identity is uncertain.
28	Observing Aquatic Environments for Toxicity	Dead fish or other aquatic animals in water may indicate toxicity.
29	Foraging Aquatic Creatures at Low Tide	Forage for clams, mussels, and crabs during low tide to access their habitats.
30	Clam Foraging Techniques	Look for clam "shows" or signs in the sand, such as small holes or water spurts.
31	Catching Crabs with Protection	Use gloves or crab lines/nets for safe crab catching.
32	Finding Water Sources	Look for converging animal tracks or flying birds to find water sources in nature.
33	Water Source Location in Hilly Areas	In hilly or mountainous areas, heading downhill often leads to water sources.

#	Techniques / Hacks	Explanation
34	Gathering Dew	Collect dew from grass and leaves using an absorbent cloth tied around ankles, then wring out the water.
35	Using Transpiration Bags for Water Collection	Tie a clear plastic bag around a leafy branch to collect condensation from plant transpiration.
36	Collecting Water from Transpiration Bags	Collect water from transpiration bags by the end of the day when temperatures drop.
37	Setting an Example in Foraging	Lead by example in following best foraging practices and respecting nature.
38	Gentle Wildlife Encounters	Be quiet and gentle around wildlife to blend in and avoid disturbing them.
39	Respecting Wildlife Space	Don't chase or follow wildlife, respect their need for space and safety.
40	Leave No Trace Principle	Ensure to carry out everything you bring in to protect wildlife and the environment.
41	Avoiding Nests and Dens	Stay away from nests or dens to prevent disturbing animals and causing mothers to abandon their young.

Resources

- Raynald Harvey Lemelin. 'The Management of Insects in Recreation and Tourism.' Cambridge University Press, 2013
- Pamela Ramirez. 'Seasonal Foraging.' Wild Foods to Forage During Different Seasons, CreateSpace Independent Publishing Platform, 2016
- Norman G. Marriott. 'Principles of Food Sanitation.' Springer Science & Business Media, 2013
- John Stevens. 'Gustavus Adolphus.' Perennial Press, 2018
- Ruth A. Etzel. 'Textbook of Children's Environmental Health.' Philip J. Landrigan, Oxford University Press, 2013
- Craig Jones. 'Foraging For Beginners: A Practical Guide To Foraging For Survival In The Wild.' Tektime, 2021
- Dr Jane Franklin. 'Comprehensive Guide to Herbal Medicine.' How Plants Extraction are Used to Treat and Prevent Disease, Amazon Digital Services LLC - Kdp, 2023
- Dr. Bharti Chaudhry. 'A Handbook of Common Medicinal Plants Used in Ayurveda.' Kojo Press, 2019
- Department of the Army. 'The Complete Guide to Edible Wild Plants.' Department Of The Army, Martino Fine Books, 2022
- Gerard Johnson. 'Foraging.' Foraging For Beginners - Your Complete Guide on Foraging Medicinal 2016
- Herbs, Wild Edible Plants and Wild Mushrooms (Foraging Guide, Foraging for Survival, Foraging Tips, Foraging Wilderness), CreateSpace Independent Publishing Platform, 2016
- Andrew Smith. 'The Oxford Encyclopedia of Food and Drink in America.' OUP USA, 2013

- Food and Agriculture Organization of the United Nations. 'Edible Insects.' Future Prospects for Food and Feed Security, Arnold van Huis, Food and Agriculture Organization of the United Nations, 2013
- Juan A. Morales-Ramos. 'Insects as Sustainable Food Ingredients.' Production, Processing and Food Applications, Aaron T. Dossey, Academic Press, 2016
- Karen Marie Ackroff. 'Foraging for Macronutrients.' Effects of Variation in the Availability and Abundance of the Protein Source, Rutgers University, 1987
- Natasha Glibber. 'Cooking With Edible Wild Plants.' Recipes For Exploring The Flavors Of Edible Wild Plants, Booktop, Amazon Digital Services LLC - Kdp, 2023
- B.J. Harrington. 'Industrial Cleaning Technology.' Springer Science & Business Media, 2013
- Emma Chapman. 'A Handbook of Scotland's Wild Harvests: The Essential Guide to Edible Species, with Recipes and Plants for Natural Remedies, and Materials to Gather for Fuel, Gardening, and Craft.' The Essential Guide to Edible Species, with Recipes and Plants for Natural Remedies, and Materials to Gather for Fuel, Gardening and Craft, Fi Martynoga, Saraband, 2012
- Karen Monger. 'Adventures in Edible Plant Foraging.' Finding, Identifying, Harvesting, and Preparing Native and Invasive Wild Plants, Simon and Schuster, 2016
- Lee Peterson. 'A Field Guide to Edible Wild Plants of Eastern and Central North America.' Houghton Mifflin Harcourt, 1978
- Thomas J. Elpel. 'Botany in a Day.' The Patterns Method of Plant Identification: Thomas J. Elpel's Herbal Field Guide to Plant Families, HOPS Press, 2004
- Simon Mayo. 'Computational Botany.' Methods for Automated Species Identification, Paolo Remagnino, Springer, 2016

- Jan Phillips. 'Wild Edibles of Missouri.' Missouri Department of Conservation, 1998
- Nuffield Council on Bioethics. 'The Ethics of Research Involving Animals.' Nuffield Council on Bioethics, 2005
- Thomas Caraco. 'Social Foraging Theory.' Luc-Alain Giraldeau, Princeton University Press, 2000
- Logan Hannah. 'Essentials of Foraging.' The Ultimate Guide to Foraging, Amazon Digital Services LLC - KDP Print US, 2021
- Tim Ingold. 'The Perception of the Environment.' Essays on Livelihood, Dwelling and Skill, Routledge, 2021
- Robert Paine. 'The Prepper's Guide to Foraging.' CreateSpace Independent Publishing Platform, 2014

Exclusive Bonuses

Dear Reader,

I am thrilled to present to you five exclusive bonuses that beautifully complement your journey into the fascinating world of foraging. These resources have been carefully curated to enhance your understanding, skills, and appreciation of the natural world around us.

Bonus 1 - Harvesting with Heart: An Ethical Foraging Guide: This comprehensive guide delves into the principles of ethical foraging, teaching you how to responsibly gather wild foods while preserving the integrity of the ecosystems you explore. It's packed with insights on sustainable harvesting techniques, legal considerations, and respect for nature.

Bonus 2 - Clues from Nature: A Crossword Journey in Ethical Foraging: Engage your mind with this unique crossword puzzle book, each themed around the world of foraging. It's not only a fun activity but also a great way to reinforce your knowledge about plant species, foraging ethics, and environmental stewardship.

Bonus 3 - Wild Bounty: A Forager's Field Notes Journal: Document your foraging adventures with this beautifully designed journal. It offers space for notes, sketches, and reflections, helping you track the plants you find, the locations you explore, and the seasons of abundance.

Bonus 4 - Foraging Words: A Nature-Inspired Word Search Adventure: Perfect for relaxing after a day of foraging, these word search puzzles are themed around plants, ecosystems, and foraging techniques. It's a delightful way to unwind while keeping your mind engaged with your newfound passion.

Bonus 5 - Nature's Pharmacy: A Forager's Guide to Medicinal Plants: Explore the healing power of nature with this guide to medicinal plants. It offers detailed profiles of various plants, their health benefits, and how to safely and ethically harvest and use them in your own home remedies.

To Access Your Bonuses:

Scan the QR Code Below: Simply use your phone's camera or a QR code reader to scan the code, and you'll be directed straight to the bonus content.

Visit the Link: Access these enriching resources by visiting this link https://bit.ly/Olsen-F

These bonuses are designed to enrich your foraging experience, deepening your connection with nature and enhancing your skills as an ethical forager.

Thank you for embarking on this enlightening journey with me. May these resources inspire you, educate you, and bring you closer to the natural world.

Warm regards,

Hugo James Olsen